H[illegible]
Spirit[illegible] Healing

Michael Bradford

HEALTH HARMONY

Note from the Publishers

Any information given in this book is not intended to be taken as a replacement for medical advice. Any person with a condition requiring medical attention should consult a qualified practitioner or therapist.

Published by: M/s B. Jain Publishers arrangement with Findhorn Press, The Park, Findhorn, Forres IV36 OTZ Scotland

Cover by: David Gregson.
Line drawings by Adrian King.
Author photograph by Findhorn Foundation Visual Arts.
Layout and setting in Garamond by Findhorn Press.

First Indian edition 1998
Reprint edition 1999, 2002

Printed in India for sale in Indian subcontinent.

Price: Rs. 100.00

Published by: Kuldeep Jain for

HEALTH HARMONY

an imprint of

B. Jain Publishers (P) Ltd.

1921, Street No. 10, Chuna Mandi,
Paharganj, New Delhi 110 055 (INDIA)
Phones: 3670430, 3670572, 3683200, 3683300
Fax: 011-3610471 & 3683400
Email: bjain@vsnl.com
Website: wwwbjainbooks.com

Printed in India by:

J.J. Offset Printers

7, Printing Press Area, Ring Road, Wazirpur, Delhi - 110 035

ISBN-81-7021-843-8

Bookcode : BN-5292

CONTENTS

ILLUSTRATIONS

FOREWORD

Anyone who has come into contact with Michael Bradford will know that he channels spiritual energy with the focus of a laser beam. This energy leaps out of every page of his book to enlighten us all about hands-on spiritual healing.

As a general practitioner I consult on a daily basis with people who are in pain — physical, mental, emotional and spiritual. My own interest in hypnotherapy has taught me a great deal about the mind-body interface. However, Michael has shown that we are not complete without spirit. His book weaves all three into one with simple techniques which are easily learned and assimilated. I commend it to anyone involved in caring for people, and especially to my medical colleagues, whose horizons are ever expanding.

Lewis Walker, MD
General Practitioner
Buckie, Scotland

Dedication

This book is dedicated to you, my brothers and sisters who are interested in learning more about healing and are committed to your own healing process.

I thank God, Holy Spirit, my spiritual guides and teachers, the healing angels and all of my earthly friends who have had faith in me, encouraged me, supported me and challenged me in my own healing process.

As each of us chooses to change and heal, I know in my heart that we automatically create ripples of healing energy, like the ripples caused by a stone landing in a still pond. These healing ripples radiate through our selves, our family, our community, our planet and our universe.

Preface

Michael Bradford is one of those special people whom you recognise immediately when you meet him. This doesn't come from having met him before, or having seen his picture, or anything in the normal realm of experience. A chiropractic intern summarised it for me the other day. He first met Michael while attending a large Native American ceremonial gathering. As Michael offered up the peace pipe to honour the Great Spirit, the young man, who sat on the opposite side of the sacred fire circle, watched through the flames as Michael transformed before his eyes. Suddenly Michael appeared to be clothed in Native American dress. The rest of the circle of participants went of focus in his vision, and for a few moments he and Michael were magically transported through the smoke hole. It was in this other world that he fully recognised Michael, and knew that they had much work to do together.

Direct knowing such as this, especially coming through a spontaneously altered state of consciousness, is a major theme of Michael's work and teaching, and the recognition many of us discover for him. Michael has dedicated his life to serving as a guide for others. By allowing spirit to flow through him, he assists us in opening ourselves to our spiritual nature and the higher spiritual guidance that is available to all of us.

In November 1991 I examined Michael's eyes as part of a routine health evaluation. When I dilated his pupils and viewed the inside of his eyes, I detected a lesion in the peripheral retina of his left eye which had the appearance of an active site of inflammation and leakage of toxic fluids into the overlying tissue. This overlying tissue, called the vitreous, appeared quite hazy and was filled with both small floaters and long strands of matter.

When I described the appearance of this area, Michael asked if we could stop and do some energy work on it. First we asked what the source of this lesion was. The answer that came through for Michael was that at the age of 3 he had swallowed a quantity of pesticides, after which his stomach was pumped.

Michael then asked if I would mind participating in a healing process for this lesion in his eye. Of course, I said I would be happy to help. As Michael led us, we visualised the area and cleaned it out energetically, a process he describes in this book. It took all of about 30 seconds. I then took a look back in the eye with the biomicroscope. To my amazement and gratification, the vitreous now appeared quite clear above the lesion. The lesion itself seemed now to be inactive. The energy I sensed from looking at it was quite peaceful as opposed to the bubbling, active sensation of a minute before.

The implications of such potentials for self-healing are as obvious as they are profound. Never before have I actually seen such a dramatic shift in the visible health of living tissue in such a brief time. As we learn to focus these abilities for ourselves, imagine what we can create together — both in terms of physical health and capabilities and in terms of wisdom and profound spiritual connections with others.

Michael has learned much through his years of exploration. In his typical manner of sharing his enthusiasm and excitement for this work, he has put together this manual to assist you in healing yourself and those around you. Together we are healing the planet, one soul at a time. This healing is not just about the physical manifestations of disease, but about a core level shift in our being. It can manifest as a new abundance of energy and vitality, as a paradigm shift in family and work relations, or simply as an inner smile that is released from somewhere deep inside. Come and join us in an exploration of life lived to its fullest. Dare to be who you truly are, for in doing so, you honour the Great Spirit in all of us.

Glen Swartwout
A.B., O.D., F.I.C.A.N., F.C.S.O.

Author's Notes

Energy is neither positive nor negative, neither good nor bad. Energy is energy. We place labels on things so we can identify and discuss them. For the sake of convenience, I have taken the liberty of categorising energy as either 'positive' or 'negative' during the discussions about healing in this book. I have chosen to use these terms solely for the purpose of simplification.

When I speak of positive energy I am referring to healing energy. This energy is pure, has a high vibrational rate and comes directly from God. The colour of this energy can be white, golden, violet, pink, blue or emerald green.

When I use the term negative energy, I am referring to trapped, blocked, discordant or disharmonious energy. This energy is generally contaminated, has a low vibrational rate, and is connected with emotional trauma, illness, dis-ease or injury. The colour of this energy can be brown, black, red, red orange or grey. Sometimes it can look murky.

The illustrations in this book use either solid or broken arrows to indicate movement. The solid lines show the physical motion of the body. Broken arrows are used to indicate the movement of energy. Please remember that these illustrations are for reference only. Always refer to the verbal description for clarification.

Many of the techniques described involve the visualisation of energy and colours. Although some people will be able to visualise clearly what is being described, others may not. If you cannot, simply allow yourself to sense the energy in any way that is comfortable for you. Follow through, trusting that regardless of what you feel, or see, the healing has taken place.

All of the techniques described in this book are done with the person fully clothed. If someone is wearing a coat, jacket or heavy sweater in addition to their regular clothing

I ask them if they would mind taking off this outer layer. Remember, energy can move easily through clothing.

In healing, no one ever knows exactly what another person really needs or what their lessons are. We, as healers, can only provide the love, support and healing energy as best we can to assist someone else in their healing process. From that point on it is up to the person receiving the healing to open to and take responsibility for their own healing process.

Please remember that healing does not always mean the person is cured. It does mean, however, that the person has changed.

INTRODUCTION

This book has evolved from my burning passion to demystify the art of healing. In my heart I know that we all have the ability to be a vehicle for healing energy and can, within a short period of time, learn to assist ourselves and others. While travelling internationally I have been amazed at the number of people I have met who have natural healing talents yet were unaware of their gifts. In almost all cases these individuals have been able to begin using their abilities in an active, conscious way with only minimal instruction.

In 1993 I spent five weeks in Bali, Indonesia, doing healing work with people who spoke little, if any, English; I speak only a few words of Indonesian. Additionally, Bali follows the Hindu religion, of which I know virtually nothing. Even these factors did not detract from the healings.

Using the techniques described in this book, I was able to work with a variety of individuals, from rice farmer to healer, with excellent results. When I visited and worked on someone I knew in a hospital, the family members of five other patients, whom I did not know and none of whom spoke any English, motioned for me to work on their loved ones. Before I left the hospital there was a marked change in each individual I assisted.

These results confirmed that these techniques work well regardless of cultural, religious or language differences. The physical body and earthly traumas are similar in all cultures; only the way people deal with them outwardly is different.

Since 1984 I have travelled throughout North America teaching people how to use healing energy. All of the techniques described in this book are the direct result of my own personal experience while teaching people how to work with healing energy and guiding thousands of private healing sessions.

The healing work I now do is an integration of Eastern

and Western healing approaches and my own techniques. This 'Core Energy Clearing' works on a person's mental, physical, emotional and spiritual levels.

The purpose of this book is to teach simple techniques whereby people can begin to sense and work with healing energy within minutes. Later chapters teach more advanced techniques. The methods and examples used have been designed so that everyone, regardless of educational or religious background or prior understanding of energy, can awaken his own natural healing abilities and become proficient in working with healing energy within a short time. In fact, the techniques are so simple that even children have learned to use them.

The youngest person ever to learn healing work from me was Kevin, a 2½ year old boy, who watched me as I worked with his mother, Jennifer. Almost immediately the boy was reaching out to people and mimicking what I had done with his mother. Even I was surprised at how strongly the healing energy came through his hands. The people he touched could feel both the heat and energy coming from them.

Often people are so filled with their own preconceived ideas, doubts and fears that they fail to listen to or accept new approaches. The tendency is to filter all new information through their past programming, and only to validate new information that conforms to previous experiences, cultural and religious backgrounds, and family values. The following parable helped me to open my mind and my heart, and encouraged me to accept new concepts that were very foreign at first.

The University Professor

A university professor once journeyed high into the mountains of Japan to speak with a particular Zen monk. Upon finding him, the professor introduced himself, listed his degrees and asked to be taught about Zen.

"Would you like some tea?" the monk asked.

"Yes, I would," the professor replied.

The old monk began pouring tea until it reached the cup's brim, then continued pouring until the tea ran over onto the table and began dripping to the floor.

"Stop! Stop!" cried the professor. "Can't you see that the cup is already full? It won't hold any more!"

The monk replied, "Like this cup, you are already full of your own knowledge and preconceptions. In order to learn, you must first empty your cup."

Please open your heart and your mind and set aside any preconceived ideas. Read this book from a place of trusting and allowing. Tremendous benefits and dramatic results can occur using the simple techniques described.

Please write to me (c/o Findhorn Press, The Park, Findhorn, Forres IV36 0TZ, Scotland) and tell me of the results you experience. Thank you.

Michael Bradford

ACKNOWLEDGEMENTS

When the idea of this book came to me in Portland, Oregon, USA in 1991, I did not have the financial resources or the typing skills to start the project. Upon praying for guidance, a number of people came forward and lovingly offered their assistance. Mary Kohnke offered a computer, Jennifer Spinner offered to do the typing and Bruce Spinner offered software consulting. With this co-creative spirit this book was started.

During the middle stage, in 1992, the men's healing group which met every week at my home assisted me in formulating my ideas. I especially wish to thank Dick Mort, Ken Berry, Dr Bob Doughton, Todd Pennington and Jay Schroder. Jay also donated countless hours editing the manuscript. Without his encouragement this book might never have been completed. Helena Wolfe assisted with the typing and editing.

The final stage was almost as challenging as the beginning. During this stage Rosalie Deer Heart, my partner, contributed endless hours editing the final draft. Her love, support and guidance were vital to the completion of this book. Mrs Anne Greaves, an intuitive artist from Scunthorpe, England, created the design for the cover of this book and directed me to add the section on Planetary Healing. Adrian King, a graphic arts student at North Lindsay College, produced the line drawings. Linda and Ken Forster assisted with typing the final draft and Angela Wright colour-coordinated the book cover.

I extend my heartfelt appreciation to Edith and Al Thomas, to Duncan and Robin Bowen and to Boyd Holloway for their steadfast love, support and encouragement for both my healing work and in writing this book. I also thank Sandra Kramer for her gentle editing and Findhorn Press for publishing my first book.

Many other people contributed to the creation of this book. I apologise that space is not available to thank each of you. Please know that I am profoundly grateful for your comments.

One

From Corporate Executive to Healer

MEXICO — THE EXPERIENCE WHICH CHANGED MY LIFE

In early Summer 1983 two friends, Peter and Michael, asked me to go on a four-month camping trip with them into the interior of Mexico. My friends are healers and offered to teach me how to work with the healing energy. I jumped at this opportunity to observe and to learn more about healing, little knowing how this trip was to change my life!

Although I had received some healing sessions and had taken a few basic lessons in using healing techniques, I rarely worked on others. I had virtually no confidence in myself and felt that I had little, if any, healing ability. Ordinarily I am not shy, but when it came to healing I felt like an insecure, scared child, afraid of doing something wrong and hurting someone.

About four weeks into the trip, we hired a guide and rented some horses to explore the back country along the continental divide. The region was extraordinarily beautiful and from time to time we would tie the horses and explore various trails that branched off the main route.

Our guide, José Vazquez (nicknamed Tito), was one of the most spiritual beings I had ever met. Everything Tito did, he did with a joy and lightness I had never seen before. It pleased me to watch him. When the horses needed to be fed, he fed them immediately; when other chores needed to be done, he did them with a zest and an ease that impressed me.

Because we had been able to rent only three horses and there were four of us, we offered to rotate the riding with

Tito. He declined, telling us he preferred to walk. Tito was quietly confident and proud without any hint of arrogance.

One afternoon we tied up the horses and he led us along a narrow walking trail. In places the trail was overgrown with vegetation which he quickly cleared away with his machete. In one area the growth was especially thick. Tito cleared enough so that my friends could pass and then he continued to trim a tree limb that hung over the trail.

At this point everyone except me had passed Tito and continued down the trail. I was tired and had stopped in the shade to rest. By chance I happened to be watching Tito as he worked on the tree limb. Tito did not realise that I had stayed behind and was watching.

I observed him swing his machete, hitting the tree limb. Then I saw the machete ricochet off the tree and hit the back of his left hand. I couldn't see any blood but I knew he was hurt by the way he grabbed his left hand and sat down on a large rock.

I sat motionless for several seconds just watching. As I watched I felt a knowing well up from deep within me. An overwhelming feeling of unconditional love and compassion picked me up and moved me from where I sat. With neither doubt nor hesitation I walked over to him, knelt down in front of him, pointed to his injured hand, and said, "Diga me (give it to me)." I couldn't speak enough Spanish to explain what I intended to do. In truth, I didn't know myself.

As he held out his injured hand I could see that the machete had not broken the skin. I put my left hand, palm down, a couple of inches above his injured hand (see Fig. 1). Then I placed my right hand, palm down, near the ground. I closed my eyes and prayed, saying. "God, please help me, please help me to help this man. This man is so beautiful. He is so gentle. Please help him." Almost instantly I felt the negative energy, his pain, being drawn out of his hand and into my left hand. It flowed up my left arm, across

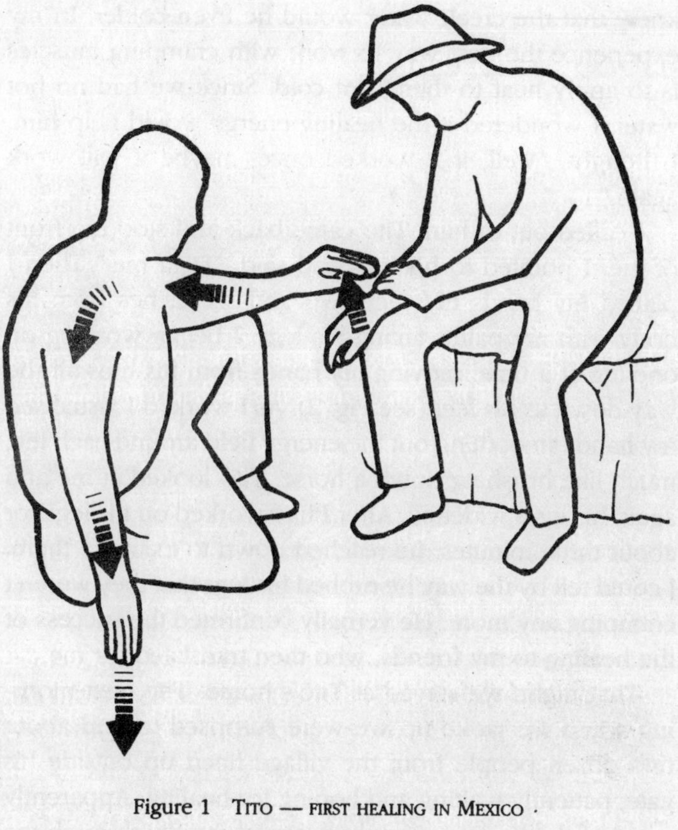

Figure 1 TITO — FIRST HEALING IN MEXICO

my body, down my right arm and out my right hand into the ground. After a moment or so he gingerly rubbed his injured hand as if searching for the pain. Then he looked at me with surprised, wide-open eyes. Intuitively I knew that healing had occurred. I nodded to him and walked down the trail to rejoin my friends.

Later that afternoon we arrived at his home, a simple adobe-brick house in a small mountain village. At dark I saw Tito take a towel and start walking down the road. I asked my friends where he was going. They translated, saying that his legs were cramping and he was going down to the creek to wash them. The night air was cold and I knew that the creek water would be even colder. In my experience the best way to work with cramping muscles is to apply heat to them, not cold. Since we had no hot water, I wondered if the healing energy would help him. I thought, "Well, if it worked once, maybe it will work again."

I called out to him. Tito came back and stood in front of me. I pointed to his legs and said, "Diga me." Then I placed my hands between two and six inches from his body with my palms facing his legs. I began working on one leg at a time, moving my hands from his hips all the way down to his feet (see Fig. 2). As I worked I visualised my hands smoothing out the energy field around each leg, much like brushing down a horse. Tito looked at me and again his eyes widened. After I had worked on his legs for about three minutes, he reached down to examine them. I could tell by the way he rubbed his legs that they weren't cramping any more. He verbally confirmed the success of the healing to my friends, who then translated for me.

That night, we stayed at Tito's home. The next morning when we woke up we were surprised to find about two dozen people from the village lined up outside his gate, patiently waiting and hoping for healing. Apparently word of the healing work had spread rapidly through the small village.

I still look back on this, my first day as a healer, with amazement; it had been so easy and natural. The results of this first healing experience were so profound and so dramatic for both of us. I am continually grateful to be able to share this magnificent gift.

My desire, my passion and my commitment are to share this gift of healing and the simple, effective techniques I have learned with all who are willing to learn and receive the benefits.

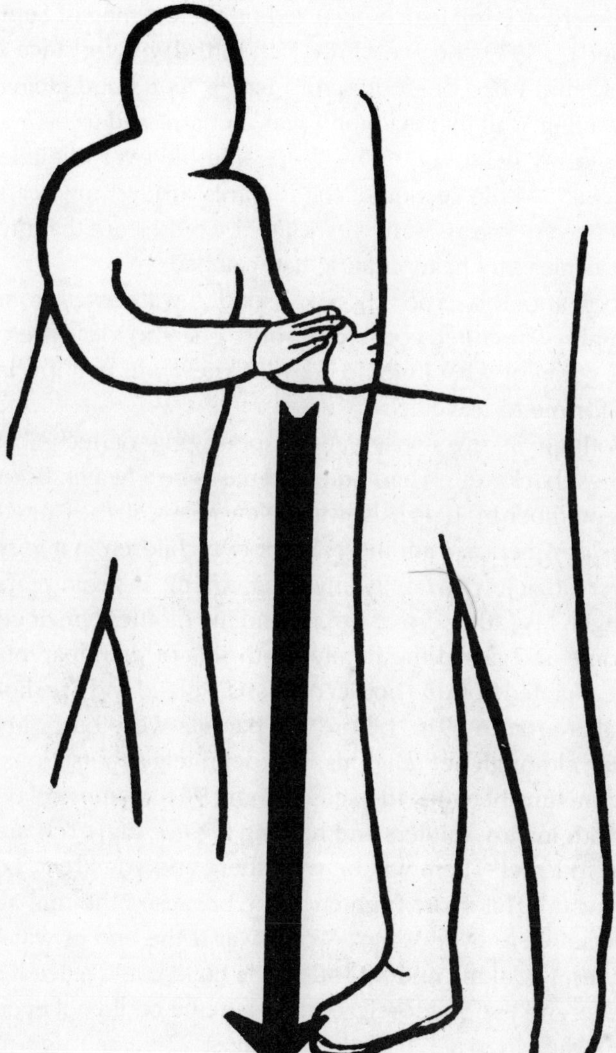

Figure 2 TITO — CRAMPING LEGS

THE PATH TO BECOMING A HEALER

The major turning point which opened the doorway for the experience in Mexico occurred on the evening of September 13, 1979, the eve of my 35th birthday. Ever since I was a child I had been drawn to Israel. As I stood facing the Wailing Wall that evening I was embarrassed to hear a voice in my head say, "Why do people die over this pile of rocks?" Within seconds I felt the area around my heart become very warm. Many years later I would learn that my heart centre, my heart chakra, had opened.

Soon after this experience I decided to walk away from the highly-structured corporate world. I had no idea where I was going or what I would do. All I knew was that it was time for me to leave.

Nothing in my conservative upbringing or technical business background had prepared me to be a healer. Born on September 14, 1944 in Newark, New Jersey, in the United States of America, I am the elder of two children in a very conservative Jewish family; my sister, Arlene, is seven years younger. My father drove a truck and my mother remained at home and raised the family. Both sets of grandparents had emigrated from the border of Russia, Poland and Czechoslovakia around 1916, before my parents were born. My family, although not religious, was definitely superstitious.

Sometime between the ages of 7 and 9 I remember playing with my toy soldiers and hearing a voice say, "You are to go to Israel. There will be wars there and you are to be a general." This voice frightened me because I thought all the wars were over! Wasn't World War II the end of wars? Besides, I couldn't understand how a child could leave his parents and live in a foreign land where he could not even speak the language. It took me almost 27 years to go to Israel and face this calling.

Leaving home shortly after finishing high school, I worked my way through college. In college I took chemical engineering for pre-med and then, after my second year, switched to a business major. In 1968 I graduated with a BBA in Business and Economics, with a minor in mathematics. In 1977 I returned to night school to obtain a Master's Degree in International Management, majoring in Japanese Studies.

From 1968 to 1980 I worked for a number of large corporations, moving further and further up the corporate ladder. I began as a sales representative for a printing company, travelling the eleven western states. Then I was Product Manager for a computer supplies corporation and, finally, the President of a $2 million manufacturing corporation employing 100 people.

After my experience in front of the Wailing Wall I started to disengage from the corporate world. At the end of 1980 this process was complete and I prayed to God, saying, "God, I surrender. Wherever You want me to go, whatever You want me to do, I am ready."

Three months later I met others on the spiritual path, including psychics and healers. During the next six years, as I travelled throughout North America, from Mexico to Alaska, I was fortunate to have the opportunity to meet and work with hundreds of healers, including Native American medicine people and various psychic surgeons trained in the Philippines. Initially I was the student. Within a few years I was able to start sharing knowledge and before long began working alongside these healers. As I gained experience and my own healing progressed, I was able to help other healers in their healing process by assisting them to identify and clear their energy blockages.

My search for healing began in 1977 when I went in for counselling to resolve my emotional pain. I was frustrated and felt a very high anxiety level. I remained in traditional therapy for three years. In 1980 I started to branch out, seeking healing from other sources. It has been the journey of my own healing which has drawn me to search out alternative healing techniques.

As I continued my healing process I was amazed to discover that I had been the victim of emotional and sexual incest and abuse as a child. My high anxiety and frustration level started to make sense. It has been my search for healing that has motivated me initially to find help for myself and then to assist others.

I have done my best to observe, ask questions and understand energetically and experientially what other healers were doing, and how and why their techniques worked, as well as noting which were the most effective methods used. These are the techniques I now share with you.

Below are additional examples of the types of healings that can be achieved.

CHARLIE'S BICYCLE ACCIDENT

In the summer of 1985, Charlie, the 15-year-old son of a friend, was riding his bicycle very fast down a steep hill when he noticed that the car just in front of him had its right turn signal on. Charlie made the assumption that the driver was planning to go down to the traffic light at the bottom of the hill before turning. Instead, the car abruptly pulled into a driveway directly in front of Charlie, cutting him off. It happened so fast that Charlie smashed into it with such force that he shattered the rear passenger window of the car, sending glass flying all over the back seat. Charlie's left shoulder was so badly bruised that the owner of the vehicle took him to the hospital for x–rays.

Shortly after Charlie returned home from the hospital, I asked him if he would like me to do some energy work with him. Charlie had no prior experience of working with healing or with energy and he was sceptical. He was in so much pain, however, that he agreed to let me work with him. I explained to Charlie that we would work together

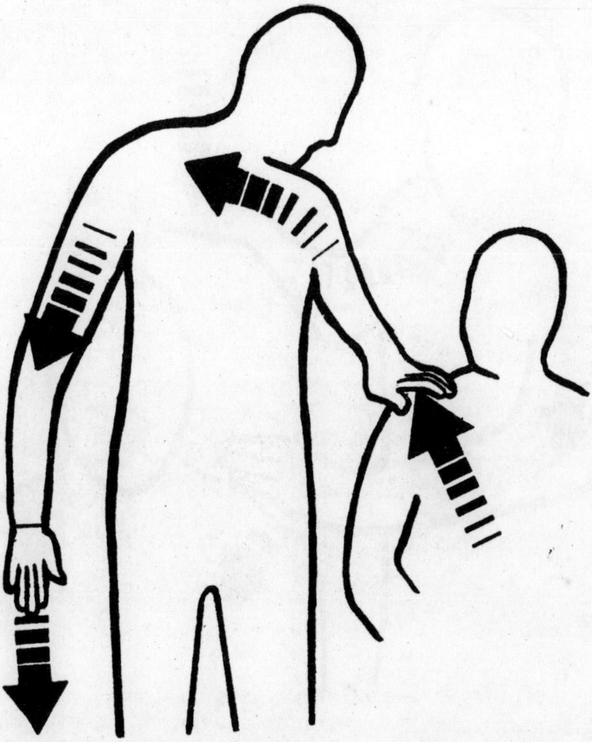

Figure 3 CHARLIE — REMOVING PAIN FROM SHOULDER

first to remove the pain and the negative energy. When that was released, we would fill the area with positive healing energy.

I rubbed my hands together to activate the healing energy and said a prayer. Then I put my left hand, palm down, about 2 inches above his bruised shoulder. I pointed my right hand down toward the earth (see Fig. 3). I then asked him to visualise a full-colour moving picture in his mind of the negative energy, the pain, coming out of his shoulder and being pulled into my left hand. Working together with Charlie, I visualised the negative energy being siphoned out from his injured shoulder and into my left

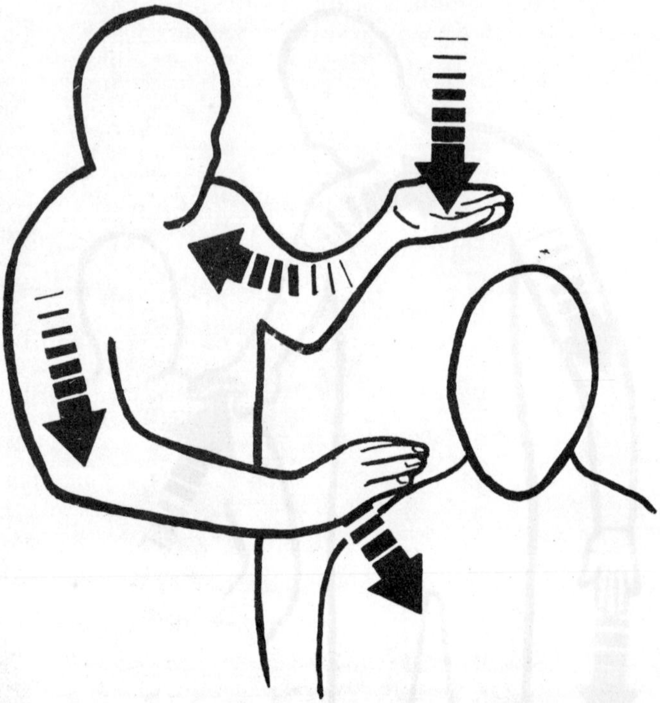

Figure 4 CHARLIE — DIRECTING HEALING ENERGY INTO SHOULDER

hand. Then we visualised it flowing through an insulated tube through my body, over to my right hand and down into the ground. As I did this I asked if he could feel the energy moving. He could. I worked for about three minutes. We both could feel a gradual decrease in the amount of negative energy being pulled off until there was little, if any, sensation of pain left.

I then took my hand from his shoulder, rubbed my hands together to activate more energy and replaced them in the same way. We repeated this process three or four more times until we could both feel the pain being drawn from his shoulder, tapering off and eventually stopping. At this point, it felt as if all the negative energy was removed from his shoulder. Charlie felt relief from the pain as this energy was drained off. I knew, however, that we had completed only half of the healing.

Then I rubbed my hands together again and said, "Okay, Charlie, we removed the negative energy. Now we're going to reverse the process and put in good energy, healing energy." I held my left hand palm up in front of me to receive positive healing energy from the universe. Then I placed my right hand palm down just over his shoulder to send this healing energy into the area that had been injured (see Fig. 4). I asked Charlie to visualise and feel the healing energy filling up, saturating and healing his shoulder. I asked him to see and feel the colour of the positive energy: emerald green, pink, or whatever colour of the rainbow he felt was the most powerful healing energy for him. Where before we were feeling the negative energy coming out, now we were feeling the healing energy going in and completely filling the injured area. We saturated the injured area three or four times until Charlie could no longer feel any more energy going in. At this point the healing was almost finished.

Most people do not realise that the auric field — the energy field around the body — experiences cuts, bruises, breaks, punctures, tears, shocks and trauma just as the physical body does. For a healing to be complete, this energy field must also be worked on.

To repair the damage done to Charlie's auric field by the impact of the accident, I visualised a soothing, healing salve in the palm of my right hand and began working about six inches from his body. As I did this I imagined myself smoothing out his energy field, as if spreading icing on a cake. The final step was to smooth the energy from the injured shoulder all the way down the arm past the fingers (see Fig. 5). During the entire process I kept asking Charlie what he was feeling and had him visualise each

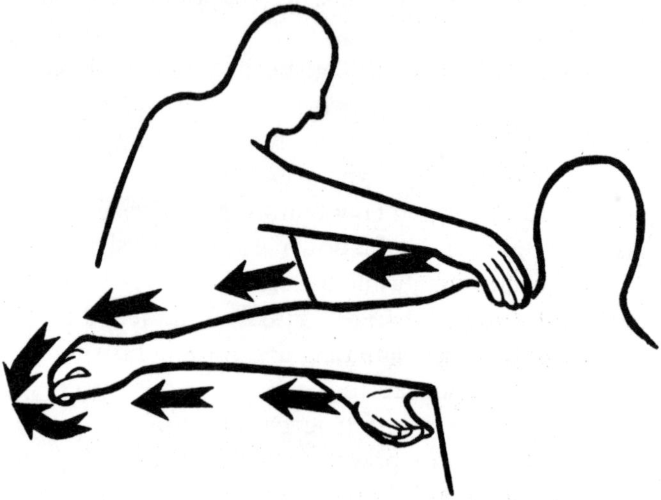

Figure 5 CHARLIE — SMOOTHING ENERGY FIELD

step with me. In the energy field directly above the injury Charlie and I could both feel a concentration of coarse, thick energy. As we smoothed out his energy field, this resistance melted away, leaving the area much clearer.

When Charlie lay down to go to sleep I talked to him in a very soft voice, telling him, "Charlie, your body is healing. It knows how to heal and it's healing right now. It's healing perfectly." I affirmed that his body knew what it needed to do to heal quickly and completely. I continued to talk with him, calming and relaxing him even more as he drifted off to sleep.

The next morning, Charlie went to work with his arm in the sling that the hospital had provided for him. By mid-morning, he was able to take off the sling and resume working without pain. To the best of my knowledge Charlie did not develop any bruises.

Results like this are possible when trust and rapport are

created, or already exist, between the healer and the person receiving the healing. Trust and rapport can usually be created within minutes if the healer listens carefully and remains non-judgemental. A safe, trusting relationship between the healer and the recipient reduces the fear, tension and resistance which can stand in the way of healing.

HEALING SUPPORT GROUP — AURA-CLEANSINGS

From 1989-92 I co–facilitated a weekly Healing Support Group in Portland, Oregon. At the end of each session we did a gentle energy balancing and aura cleansing on each person who requested it. Each aura cleansing lasted a maximum of 10 minutes. There were two incidents which stand out in my memory.

The first was with a woman I had never met before who appeared to be in her late 60s or early 70s. Before I started working with her I asked her how I could assist her. She told me that she was going across the country, to the East Coast, to be treated for cancer and asked that I do some energy work on her. After the aura cleansing she looked deeply into my eyes and told me this was the first time in her entire life that she had ever felt and known peace. She was so thankful. I never saw or heard from her again.

Another woman in her late 20s was sitting in the circle surrounding the area where we were doing aura cleansings. She was about three feet away from me, facing the centre of the circle where four or five of us were doing aura cleansings. At the end of the healing session she shared that some time previously she had been in an auto accident and had suffered a neck injury that had not healed properly and had continued to bother her. She said that while I was working on someone else she felt a bolt of energy shoot down through the top of her head and into her neck. Then she felt her neck pop and realised that it had been totally healed.

CHILDREN WITH FEVER

In Canada during the summer of 1986, and again in Palm Springs, California during the winter of 1991, I had the opportunity to work with children less than a year old who had fevers in excess of 104 degrees.

The first child, in Jasper, British Columbia, was about six months old. His fever had come on suddenly, causing the mother to be very concerned. The child I worked on in Palm Springs, California was ten months old and had been running a fever exceeding 104 degrees for more than twelve hours. Because this fever occurred over the Christmas holidays, the child's doctor was unavailable.

In both of these situations I used exactly the same approach. As I worked with each child, my first objective was to remove the excess energy, the heat, around the body and lower the fever. To do this I did a quick aura cleansing similar to the one I did with Charlie.

My intention here was to remove the excess heat as fast as possible. Visualising my hands as giant brushes I quickly brushed their energy field from head to toe at least a half dozen times until I could feel their temperature dropping.

After removing the excess heat I sensed their body energy to find the hottest area. Because a baby is so small, pinpointing the exact area is not as important as when working with an adult. In both cases I focused on the chest and stomach area. Here, as with Charlie's shoulder, I used my left hand to pull out the negative energy creating the fever and ran it through an insulated tube over to my right hand which directed it into the ground. I repeated this three or four times until the negative energy tapered off and stopped.

Next I rubbed my hands together and held my left hand up to receive healing energy and placed my right hand just above their chest area. Again I repeated sending in the positive healing energy three or four times until the baby seemed filled. To complete the healing I did a gentle aura cleansing to smooth out their energy fields.

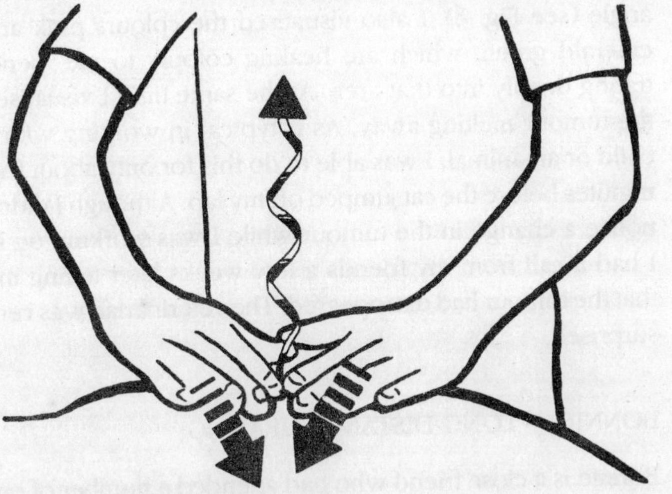

Figure 6 CAT — FORMING A TRIANGLE

Using this approach, I was able to pull out the negative energy, to smooth out the energy field around the baby, and to help break the fever. In each case, the baby's temperature dropped within 15 minutes from when I started the treatment. This approach has proved effective on many other illnesses and injuries.

CANCEROUS TUMOUR

In 1986, while visiting a friend and his wife, they told me their cat had been diagnosed by the veterinarian as having a cancerous tumour. The tumour, located on the cat's side, felt like a small lump about half an inch in size. I asked if I could work on the cat and they agreed. After activating my hands by rubbing them together I placed the cat on my lap. I gently placed my hands palms down on the cat, forming a triangle over the area of the tumour. I then visualised the healing energy coming through the palms of my hands into the cat and the negative energy, the tumour, leaving the cat through the centre of the triangle (see Fig. 6). I also visualised the colours pink and emerald green, which are healing colours to me, penetrating deeply into that area. At the same time I visualised the tumour melting away. As is typical in working with a child or an animal, I was able to do this for only about five minutes before the cat jumped off my lap. Although I didn't notice a change in the tumour while I was working on it, I had a call from my friends a few weeks later telling me that the tumour had disappeared. The veterinarian was very surprised.

BONNIE — LONG-DISTANCE HEALING

Bonnie is a close friend who had attended a number of my seminars. She and her boyfriend are on a spiritual path and always do their best to help those with whom they come in contact.

Working as both a bartender and a cocktail waitress, Bonnie was able to reach and to counsel many people who were in need. One evening Bonnie called from work. She said she was frustrated and depressed and was having trouble functioning. Bonnie told me she could not stay on the phone long and asked for my help in clearing her energy field. I agreed, telling her I would start working on her as soon as we got off the phone.

Later that evening she called to say thank you, adding that she had felt the energy shift shortly after we hung up. To this day, I have not told her that I was distracted shortly after the phone call and did not 'consciously' work on her. Apparently my agreement to participate allowed my subconscious and superconscious mind to proceed with the healing. Bonnie's request and her receptivity to the healing energy, in addition to her trust and expectation, made it possible for the healing to occur.

R.T. — LONG-DISTANCE HEALING

R.T., a conservative business associate, telephoned me long distance from his work place. During the course of the conversation, he mentioned that he had hurt his back while doing yard work that weekend and wished I lived closer so that I could do some healing work on it.

I told him I could work on him right then if he had time. He questioned whether it was possible to do healing in this manner and I assured him it was. He was surprised at first and then asked me to wait while he closed the door to his office. When he returned, I asked him to sit back in his chair, close his eyes, relax and visualise the negative energy, the pain, melting and draining from his body down into the floor. As we talked we both visualised the process occurring. He told me he could actually feel the pain leaving. Then I asked him to feel positive healing energy and to see the colours emerald green, gold, pink and/or violet filling up and saturating the sore areas. Finally we visualised his energy field being smoothed out from head to toe. After less than 5 minutes of using these visualisations healing took place. R.T. reported a substantial reduction in pain and much greater mobility. The pain did not return.

DRAMATIC HEALINGS

On two occasions I was involved with healings that fall into the category of complete or miracle healings. Each time the healing achieved was so dramatic that the recipient and I were both amazed. In the first case I had no conscious intention of doing a healing and had not realised that healing had occurred.

In 1987, during the time of the Harmonic Convergence, Eagle Feather, a medicine woman in Sedona, Arizona was leading a number of Native American ceremonies. Eagle Feather had such severe problems with her legs that at times she could not walk unassisted, having to use crutches or be carried. From the first time I met her, I honoured her for the work she was doing. Yet I could not understand how a person who was helping so many other people and working with the medicine of the Native American people could be so ill and crippled herself. In my mind and in my heart, I started calling her Dancing Legs, holding the vision of her in a state of perfect health. Whenever I saw her, I repeated the name Dancing Legs in my mind, and smiled inside.

About three weeks after I met her, I attended a Sunrise Medicine Wheel ceremony Eagle Feather was leading. When the ceremony was over, approximately three hours later, the participants all exchanged hugs. As Eagle Feather and I hugged, I instinctively placed my right hand at the base of her spine and my left hand at the top of her spine just below her neck. We hugged for only a moment and, as we hugged, she went limp in my arms. Although I was aware of her going limp, I was not consciously aware that a healing had taken place. I didn't think anything of it; I just noticed she had relaxed in my arms. A moment later, we finished our hug and went our separate ways. Later that day, a number of people came over to me to thank me for the healing I had done on Eagle Feather. On a conscious level I was totally unaware of what had transpired and could not understand what the people were thanking me for. All I knew was that I felt a lot of sincere love, honour and compassion for this woman. Holding the love and respect in my heart for her and creating the visualisation of her 'Dancing Legs' was actually the start of the healing energy I was sending her. The hug and her collapse in my arms was the completion of the healing.

Two weeks later, Eagle Feather and I went disco dancing together. According to the information she gave me, her medical doctor said that her nervous system and her muscles were healing and repairing themselves. The vision

I held of her as 'Dancing Legs' became a reality.

The healing that took place with Eagle Feather helped me to look upon the 'power of a hug' in a new way. I now realise that every time I give someone a hug, or come in contact with a person, my energy might be assisting them to heal. Just sharing love with someone can have a major impact on their transformation. Later I learned that Eagle Feather had been praying and preparing for this healing for some time and had asked the Great Spirit to work through the appropriate person to help her. I felt that her asking and being willing to receive, combined with her active preparation, contributed to the degree of healing achieved.

Another factor that played an important part in this healing was that both Eagle Feather and I had the 'creative intention' for her to heal. She had actively prayed for the healing and I had actively held the vision in my mind of her as 'Dancing Legs', already whole and healed. Our combined desire and focus were the key factors in the degree of healing which occurred.

The second dramatic healing occurred in the Spring of 1991 while we were doing aura cleansings at the close of the healing support group I co–facilitated. We were offering aura cleansings as a way of clearing out negative energy and balancing the energy field around the body. A woman I had never met requested an aura cleansing. When I asked how I could assist her, she told me she was suffering from Chronic Fatigue Syndrome (known as ME in the UK) and that her liver was hardly functioning. During the healing session, she and I were aware of the intensity of the healing energy. I remember becoming lightheaded and breaking out in a sweat as the energy flowed through my body.

After the meeting ended, she told me that she had been under medical care for some time. In addition to working with traditional medical approaches, she was actively meditating, taking special Chinese herbs, reading self-help books, visualising herself getting better and doing everything in her power to take care of herself.

She had been unable to work for so long that her long-term disability insurance was running out. To make matters worse, she was in danger of being fired by her employer. After the healing session, she made a dramatic recovery and was able to return to full-time work within a few months and to perform her duties well.

I share these stories because in my heart I know everyone is a healer. When you allow healing energy to flow through you, there is much you can do to assist others in their healing process. Remember, I was once doubtful and fearful myself. Through a willingness to trust, learn and experiment, I now trust my ability to use healing energy to help myself and others. All you require is the desire and willingness to read this book and start practising! With practice your skills will increase quickly.

Two

UNDERSTANDING ENERGY

WHAT IS HEALING ENERGY?

All of us are familiar with various forms of energy, such as magnetism, electricity and both light and heat from the sun. Another common form is electromagnetic energy which is produced when electricity is passed through a wire coil, creating a magnetic field.

Healing energy can be described as bio-electromagnetic energy because it seems to carry an electrical charge, to have magnetism and to be produced naturally by the human body. Some people can literally see this energy as colours, others hear it as sounds, and almost everyone can feel it.

Most people take for granted the various uses of electricity, magnetism and light in their everyday lives, yet these forms of energy are still not completely understood by the scientific community. Scientists have formulated the particle theory and the wave theory which both describe how light works under very different sets of conditions. However, they still cannot explain why light reacts the way it does under these different conditions. The same holds true for electricity and magnetism. People know how they react under different circumstances and have learned how to measure and to utilise them, but they still cannot explain the 'whys' of these energies.

Likewise, healing energy has been used in almost all cultures and countries since the beginning of time, yet it is not totally understood. Both past history and current successes support the existence of such energy and the many benefits of using it. Generally, these benefits and successes have been downplayed, discounted, suppressed and ignored by many in the traditional medical field. Unfortunately, the scientific community has led us into a more left–brain, traditional, scientific and medical approach to researching and studying healing energy rather than allowing themselves to be challenged and to be encouraged to research and document its benefits. Healing energy is used in many methods of healing that are labelled 'alternative' by the traditionalists.

Energy is always present, no matter where we are. The more sensitive we are to energy, the easier it is to feel it. Someone who is sensitive to energy can enter a room and feel whether the energy in the room is positive or negative, happy or sad. We either feel relaxed and comfortable with the energy around us or we do not.

Healing energy resembles the flow of water. If the person receiving the healing is open and receptive, the energy will flow easily to them. If they are resistant or fearful, the energy flow will be restricted and may just trickle.

SOURCES OF HEALING ENERGY

There are three distinct categories of healing energy. One is personal energy — the energy generated by the body. The Chinese call this Chi (chee), and the Japanese call it Ki (key). The second type is psychic energy. This is the ability to focus the power of the mind and to direct and concentrate energy through thought. The third is spiritual or mystical energy. With mystical energy, you are working with God, Spirit and the power of prayer. Here, you are going beyond your own personal power and tapping into the power of the universe.

For those who have strong personal energy and have developed good psychic abilities, it is sometimes a challenge to go beyond the personal ego and to request and accept God's help.

Using only your personal energy limits the scope and

amount of energy available to do healing. There are drawbacks also to using psychic energy. When using personal or psychic healing power without the benefit of spiritual assistance, there is a possibility you may feel tired or drained if you do a great deal of energy work. You might also become agitated or develop headaches. This is especially true when you concentrate intensely and focus your mind.

In working with mystical energy, however, the energy available is limitless. By requesting and using universal energy, you personally can achieve a much higher vibrational level and you can create a much stronger energy field for use in healing. All of my healing work is done in conjunction with God's guidance and assistance — that is, in cooperation with the positive force of universal energy. When you allow yourself — your ego self — to step aside and let the universal energy flow naturally through you, the healings that can occur are far beyond what you would normally believe possible.

It helps to keep the following ideas in mind when preparing to do healing work. Remain free of your expectations and desires, stay open to receiving the universal energy, and love, honour and respect the person who is asking for healing. The more you can do these things, the better the chance that a healing will occur.

HOW IS HEALING ENERGY TRANSFERRED?

Healing energy can be transferred by various methods, one of which is through your hands. The hands are an excellent vehicle because they can be seen, the energy can be readily felt, and this approach is acceptable to most people.

Over the years, as I continued to work with healing energy, I began to experience the energy being transferred in various surprising ways that were different to what I had expected or previously experienced

The most dramatic experience for me was the time I felt

the healing energy coming out of my eyes. This first happened in 1986 at a workshop I was giving. Other people in the room were also able to sense and feel the energy. To me it felt like waves of energy flowing from my eyes. The idea of looking into someone's eyes while talking with them took on a whole new level of importance. I realised that just by looking directly into another person's eyes, I could help them to heal and could encourage them to stay more focused and keep their attention in the present.

As I became more accepting and loving of myself, I discovered I was able to look more deeply into the eyes of others and to assist them in learning to love and accept themselves more. From this I developed a greater understanding of compassion.

Healing takes place on many levels and in many different ways. A second unexpected way of transferring energy occurred when I experienced healing energy coming through my voice. Whenever I speak in a soft, low voice the energy changes, both in the room and within the person or group I am talking with. When this happens, the energy intensifies and the opportunity for healing becomes greater. Realising these changes helped me to view praying aloud and singing with a new perspective. Even public speaking has taken on a new meaning. Through the vibrations you create with your voice, you can change the energy in a room or building and can soothe and heal yourself and others. Through consciously modulating your voice, you can encourage, support and share love. A mother's lullaby to a child is remembered for a lifetime!

Due to my technical background one of the methods of energy transfer most difficult for me to accept was visualisation, mind–to–mind healing and long–distance healing. I could easily accept the concept of healing energy when I actually felt it and could instantly see results. To accept that healing could occur even at long distances by merely closing my eyes, praying and seeing the changes for a person was a real stretch for me. With time I learned that whenever the healer or the person receiving the healing is able to visualise the change, that change has a much greater chance of occurring. When both work and visualise together, the potential for positive results is greatly multiplied. It was only after repeated successes that I began to accept that by changing my thoughts or visualisations I could change my health and my life.

EXAMPLES OF ENERGY LOCKED IN THE BODY

Energy can be locked in the body in many different ways. It can be locked in on a mental, physical, emotional or spiritual level, or in any combination of these levels. The techniques outlined in this book can help you get in touch with and unblock these energies.

On a physical level, the body absorbs and retains chemicals and unresolved emotions in the cells, muscles, bones and organs. On a mental and emotional level, there are times when memories and emotions which were either suppressed or forgotten are re-experienced and remembered as an individual is receiving a healing. If you accept that the body, mind and spirit of a person are always seeking a return to wholeness, it is easier to understand how the healing energy can assist a person in triggering and releasing these blockages. The extra energy provided in a healing session can release trauma locked in the body from accidents, abuse, fear, or loss of a family member or pet. Following are a few examples of situations that illustrate some of my experiences with blocked energy.

In 1982-83 I received some very deep massage sessions during which a number of amazing things happened. As the massage therapist was working on my legs, we both began to smell a strong odour which neither of us could identify. The smell was vaguely familiar, yet I could not put my finger on what it was. Days later, I realised that the odour was the same as the liniment I had used to help relieve leg cramps when I was running cross-country in high school. After 21 years of being trapped in my body, these chemicals were now being released. Their unmistakable odour was clearly identifiable. A similar situation occurred when the therapist was massaging the inside of my mouth around my gums and teeth; I could taste and smell Novocain. This happened a long time after my last visit to the dentist.

Chemicals, drugs, alcohol and food contaminants remain in the body much longer than most of us realise. People with a strong physical constitution can handle a greater quantity of pollution in their body before their health becomes adversely affected. Those with a very sensitive or weak constitution might instantly feel the impact of these toxins. Often, however, we are unaware of the quantity of chemicals being ingested and absorbed into our body, or the effects they can have. The cleaner the air we breathe, the purer the water we drink and the better the food we eat, the easier it is for our body to remain healthy day in and day out. A healthy body can heal more quickly, sustain more stress and deal with greater emotional and mental pressures. In addition, a physically healthy person is more likely to be mentally, emotionally and spiritually healthy than someone who is physically ill.

> *NOTE: 12-Step Programme*
> *For those who are enrolled in a 12-Step Programme for addictions and who are in the recovery process, the techniques described in this book can effectively help to break the old patterns. In addition, working with the healing energy can assist in the release of chemicals, as well as the pain and suffering associated with them.*

Blocked energy can take the form of trauma, fear, anger, hurt, grief, shame, guilt, pain, shock or resentment. Childhood traumas, events that happened or even words that were said a long time ago, can hurt and carry through into adulthood, robbing us of our aliveness and spontaneity. Children raised in homes where alcoholism, drug abuse, sexual abuse or other kinds of abuse occurred develop coping methods in order to survive. These coping methods, while helping a person survive childhood, often lead to or develop into problems as these children become adults. It is not uncommon for people raised in an emotionally abusive household either to shut down emotionally or to become abusers themselves, or both.

When emotional pain becomes so great that a person is unable to deal with it, they tend to shut down and pretend it isn't there. They might also lash out at others, sometimes without knowing why. There is a tendency to store the energy of an unresolved trauma by locking it in the body. Even if the situation happened only once, an unreleased and unresolved trauma can become trapped within the body and its energy field, causing tension, stress and possibly disease.

As a person gets in touch with a past trauma, they might cry or even become hysterical while the energy is being released. Some emotional release is to be expected. If you are working with someone who is releasing, simply stay with them and encourage them to feel the pain or trauma and express it. Releasing this stored, suppressed or blocked energy is a healthy, natural process that allows a person to resolve issues and to become more alive. Talk gently and be supportive. The energy-clearing techniques described in this book will help heal the emotions and can make a profound difference in a person's ability to function.

Negative mental energy — negative thought patterns — can be described as limiting thoughts, attitudes and belief systems that someone has placed in their mind or that have been handed down by the family or culture over generations. Prejudice and bigotry fall into this category. Feuds have held people in bondage in Europe, the Middle East and many other parts of the world. All people have been influenced by authority figures, religion, politics, social customs, marketing and advertising campaigns and by their parents. Negative thought patterns can often be recognised in people suffering from poor self-image and low self-esteem. Affirmations, which will be discussed later, are a good way to change negative thought patterns into positive ones. As we become more positive in our thinking, we heal, allowing more room for love, peace, joy and acceptance in our lives.

CHAKRAS

Chakra is a Hindu word meaning 'wheel'. The ancient Indian mystics saw the chakra centres of the body as whirling, wheel-like vortices of energy. There are seven major chakras or energy centres and many minor or lesser ones. The minor chakras include the palms of the hands and the bottoms of the feet.

The seven major chakras are located within the physical body just in front of the spine; they are aligned vertically up and down the spine. Each chakra resonates to a musical note and has associated with it a colour and an organ or gland.

When these energy centres are clear and aligned, the energy flows freely up and down the spine and throughout the nervous system, resulting in a feeling of peaceful well-being. We express ourselves through these energy centres. The chakras, as well as our physical and emotional bodies, can hold trapped negative energy. Once tension, trauma, fears and anxiety are released from the chakra system, the mental, physical, emotional and spiritual bodies heal also. The chakra system and the mental, physical, emotional and spiritual bodies are directly related. When either one is cleared the other automatically clears. It is not critical where the healing process starts or what is worked with first as much as is making the commitment and starting.

The Root Chakra, located at the base of the spine, is the chakra closest to the earth and is related to grounding and survival. When blocked this chakra contains fear and the 'fight or flight' mechanism. Healing this chakra releases fear, allows us to feel safer and assists us to remain centred and grounded. This chakra relates to the bladder, sexual organs, reproduction, sexuality, survival, safety, strength and groundedness. It resonates to the note 'C' and is perceived as the colour red.

The Spleen Chakra, the second chakra, is located near the navel. This chakra relates to power and will. Healing the second chakra releases feelings of being powerless and out of control, as well as the need to dominate and control others. When the second chakra is in balance, we feel in control of our life and we use our power gently and appropriately for the common good of all. This chakra relates to the lower intestine, adrenals, kidneys, intimacy, feelings, energy level, appetite and immunity. It resonates to the note 'D' and is perceived as the colour orange.

The Solar Plexus Chakra, the third chakra, is located at the base of the sternum and contains our emotional sensitivity and issues of personal power. Described another way, it is the chakra of our self-image and self-esteem. All personal feelings are located in this chakra centre. When it is in balance, we have clear thinking, confidence, personal power and we learn easily. When out of balance this chakra can contain anger, hostility and even rage. It creates more problems than any of the other chakras because it reflects our emotional being. It relates to the liver, spleen, stomach, gall bladder and pancreas. It resonates with the note 'E' and is perceived as the colour yellow.

The Heart Chakra, the fourth chakra, is located at the heart and relates to empathy, compassion, love and harmony. The more clear and open this chakra is, the greater the capacity to give and receive unconditional love. This chakra relates to the heart, lungs, chest area, thymus, blood and circulatory system and affects the immune and endocrine systems. It resonates with the note 'F' and is perceived as the colour emerald green.

The Throat Chakra, the fifth chakra, is located at the throat and is related to expression through communication. Fear, anxiety or trauma can cause this chakra to become restricted or to close down. When this occurs we are unable to express ourselves clearly and in severe situations may even become speechless. As we heal judgement, criticism and fear of communication, the voice becomes fuller, clearer and deeper. This chakra relates to the mouth, throat, thyroid gland, bronchial tubes, ears and nose. It resonates with the note 'G' and is perceived as the colour blue.

The Third Eye or Brow Chakra, the sixth chakra, is located in the centre of the forehead slightly above the eyebrows. This chakra is related to idealism and imagination. If we can dream it or see it, we can create it. Some forms of psychic healing are done by sending out an energy ray from this centre. The third eye, when developed, gives us the psychic ability to see beyond the physical realms — into other dimensions. This chakra aids us in looking deep within to evaluate where we are on the path of healing and spiritual growth. It relates to the thalamus and pituitary glands, ears, nose, eyes and lower brain. It resonates to the note 'A' and is perceived as the colour indigo.

The Crown Chakra, the seventh chakra, is located at the top of the head and is the connection to God, the higher self and spirit. When this chakra is clear, we are in harmony with ourselves, spirit and other people. Love, peace of mind and connection to spirit are the positive qualities of this chakra. This chakra integrates the human with the Divine and is associated with divine purpose and a person's destiny. It also goes beyond language, time and space. The crown chakra relates to the top of the head, the pituitary and pineal glands and the higher brain. It resonates with the note 'B' and is perceived as the colour violet.

Chakra	**Location**	**Gland**	**Colour**	**Note**
7 Crown	top of head	pituitary & pineal	violet	B
6 Brow/ 3rd eye	forehead between eyebrows	pituitary	indigo	A
5 Throat	throat	thyroid	blue	G
4 Heart	heart	thymus	green	F
3 Solar plexus	base of sternum	pancreas	yellow	E
2 Spleen	spleen/navel	adrenal	orange	D
1 Root/base	base of spine	gonads	red	C

Because the chakras are all connected, as are the mental, physical and emotional bodies, whenever we work with one area the entire system is affected. In addition, the chakras might contain the colours of other chakras as the issues being dealt with affect more than one area. An example of this would be a person who was sexually abused as a child. Here all of the chakras are affected.

Root chakra	sexuality, survival, safety
Second chakra	issues with power
Third chakra	issues with self-image, self-esteem
Heart chakra	issues of trust and love
Throat chakra	issues with safety of speaking out
Third eye chakra	issues with seeing and admitting what is happening or has happened
Crown chakra	issues of worthiness and trusting God

THE AURA

Everything in the universe is composed of energy and everything has an energy field around it. Plants, animals, minerals, trees and humans all have energy fields around them. This energy field, although invisible to the naked, untrained eye, extends outward from the object and is called the aura or auric field. The aura, in many ways, is much like the earth's atmosphere: densest closer to the surface, then becoming progressively less dense the farther it extends outward. All energy fields have many levels, just as the earth has many atmospheric levels.

In people, this energy field can be felt from one to three feet or more out from the physical body. Depending upon a person's energy level and level of spiritual development the aura can extend out over 50 feet from the body. The energy of a great master or teacher can be felt at even greater distances. Most of the paintings of holy people, saints and spiritual leaders depict a bright glow around their bodies, especially their heads. This glow perfectly depicts a well-developed energy field or aura.

The aura can be detected in a number of ways, including thermography, aura readings, Kirlian photography and dowsing devices. Each of these methods of detection confirms the existence of an aura around the body. Thermography is a traditional medical procedure that creates an exaggerated colour image by measuring the subtle heat patterns around the body. A healthy body emits a specific colour pattern. When a person is ill or diseased, distortions and discolorations in the colour pattern can be detected. These colour differences give clues to the degree and location of an illness, such as cancer, long before it can be detected in the physical body by other traditional diagnostic methods.

Kirlian photography generates a specific type of photograph taken within an electrical field which helps capture distinct energy fields on film. This process is so sensitive that it will even pick up the 'memory' or phantom energy image of a limb that has recently been amputated or the image of the removed portion of a leaf that has recently been cut in half.

Dowsing rods and other dowsing devices also can be used to sense the auric field around the body. In the hands of an experienced dowser these devices are extremely accurate. I have seen them respond to the energy field around a person when 25 feet or more from the physical body. Dowsing rods also can detect subtle shifts in someone's energy field as their thinking changes. If they are thinking happy thoughts, the aura expands. When they are thinking negative thoughts or they are sick, sad, angry or depressed, the energy field will contract.

Aura readings can also be done by those with psychic or intuitive sight. By reading breaks, distortions and discolorations in the energy field, some psychics can with a great deal of accuracy detect and predict what type of illness will develop, how soon it will occur and even estimate what its severity will be.

The aura can develop holes, breaks, tears and areas of dark, stagnant energy, much like the smog, pollution and holes in the ozone layer of the earth's atmosphere.

It is best if the auric field is periodically cleansed and mended, especially after a person has experienced a trauma, such as surgery or an accident. This will repair the breaks and tears that can cause energy disruptions, imbalances and leakages.

We can strengthen our body and energy field through meditation, prayer, affirmations, good diet and exercise. The energy field can be cleansed by receiving an aura cleansing or receiving healing work. You can also cleanse your own energy field by taking a hot bath with either a cup of apple cider vinegar or a cup of epsom salts added to the bath water. These help to neutralise negative energy and to balance the energy field.

Three

Sensing Energy

THE POWER OF PRAYER

Prayer, the calling in of God, Holy Spirit, Jesus, Mother Mary, the Great Spirit or Universal Energy, assists you in aligning your energies directly with the Source, thereby bypassing the ego and personality. This also takes you beyond your personal energies and psychic abilities.

The following exercise is an experiment with the power of prayer.

Exercise—Sit quietly by yourself or with a group of friends and allow yourself to relax and quiet your mind. Make sure your legs are uncrossed and your feet are flat on the floor (taking your shoes off helps even more). This keeps the energy flowing smoothly. Take a few minutes to relax and sense the energy around you. Use all your senses to feel, hear and become aware of the energy level in the room.

Now repeat the Lord's Prayer aloud three times.

Our Father, who art in heaven,
Hallowed be Thy name.
Thy kingdom come,
Thy will be done,
On earth as it is in heaven.
Give us this day our daily bread.
And forgive us our debts,
as we have forgiven our debtors.
And lead us not into temptation,
but deliver us from evil.
For Thine is the kingdom,
and the power, and the glory, forever. Amen.

Now again sit quietly and sense the energy around you. Can you see, sense, feel and/or hear a difference in the energy of the room, in the air around you and in yourself? If in a group, have each person share what they felt and then, as a group, discuss the experience.

After participating in this exercise, most people describe themselves as feeling more peaceful and experiencing a general sense of well-being. In addition, they also sense changes in the energy of the room: the energy becomes more harmonious and a higher vibration is experienced. People have also described the energy as lighter and happier.

An additional exercise is to repeat the above, saying 'Om' aloud three times instead of the Lord's Prayer.

ACTIVATING YOUR HANDS

In the middle of each palm is an energy centre, a minor chakra, which when open allows healing energy to flow either into or out of the palm (see Fig. 7). These energy centres can be used to receive energy or send energy. The left hand is for either receiving positive energy from the universe or drawing negative energy out of a person. The use of the left hand can change during a healing session. The right hand is for sending and directing energy (see Figs. 3 & 4, pp 27 & 28). In terms of polarity, the left hand has a negative electrical charge and the right hand has a positive electrical charge.

Since we want to be sending out healing energy only when it is needed, I have developed what I consider to be a fast and effective way of activating the healing energy within my body: I clap my hands together a couple of times and then vigorously rub my palms together. Either or both of these actions will work. While doing this I ask that universal healing energy start flowing through me. In my mind, I concentrate on activating the energy and visualise healing energy moving through my body. Within seconds I can

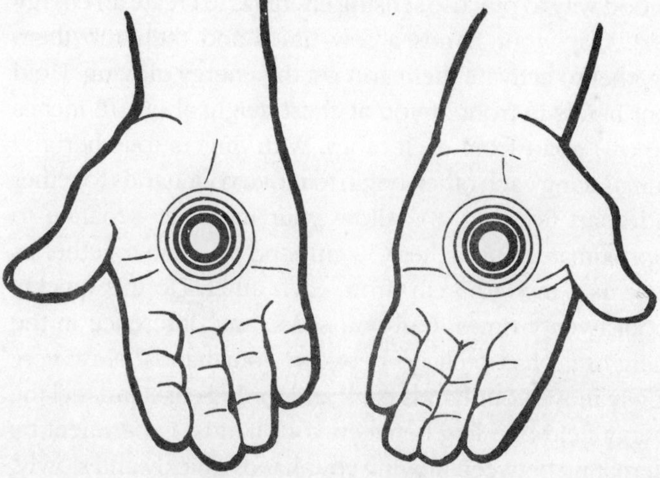

Figure 7 HANDS — ENERGY CENTRES

feel my hands becoming warm and starting to tingle as the healing energy begins to move.

There are times when I can feel my hands activate themselves when someone asks for help or is telling me about a person who is in need of help. At these times my hands respond almost instantly, becoming activated without any conscious effort or action on my part. I can literally feel my entire body shift into a healing mode. As my hands become activated, the palms become hot as the healing energy begins to flow. I can also feel the healing energy begin to radiate from my entire body. When you are committed to helping people heal, you become a vehicle for healing energy.

To rub your hands together or to clap your hands to activate the energy is not really necessary. However, this method may prove helpful until you develop your own approach to activating the flow of energy.

CREATING AN ENERGY FIELD — AN EXERCISE

A good way to practise sensing energy is to create an energy field. Clap your hands a few times and then rub them together to activate them and get the energy moving. Hold your hands in front of you at chest height about 18 inches (50 cm) apart from each other. With fingers together and palms facing each other, begin to move your hands together and apart (see Fig. 8). Allow your hands to separate to approximately 18 inches (50 cm) and to come together as close as 1 inch (2.5 cm) from each other. Do this quickly about twenty times. Can you sense any difference in the energy that has built up between your hands? Now very slowly move your hands back and forth. Sense and feel the energy field building between your hands. Experiment by alternating between moving your hands quickly and slowly. Can you feel your hands and the energy field tingling, pulsating or vibrating? Can you feel heat coming from the energy field between your hands? Does the energy have a texture to it? As you bring your hands closer together, can you feel resistance as if you were compressing something? As you move your hands farther apart, can you feel a decrease in the density of the energy field? Can you sense any other changes in the energy field? Is there any movement within it? Can you sense any colours? What other information are you aware of?

CREATING AN ENERGY BALL — AN EXERCISE

Activate the healing energy by clapping and rubbing your hands together. Hold your hands in front of you at the height of your chest with your palms facing each other. Curve your hands slightly as if holding a large ball. Now move your hands together until they are about an inch (2.5 cm) apart, and then farther apart until they are about 18 inches (50 cm) away from each other. Move your hands

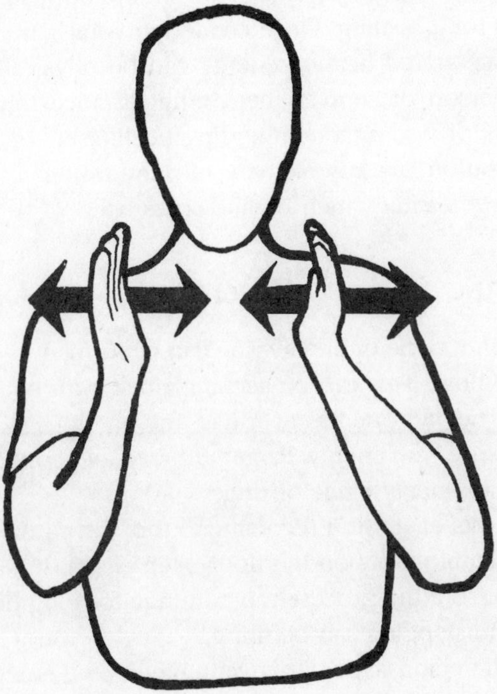

Figure 8 CREATING AN ENERGY FIELD

slowly back and forth and feel the energy building in intensity. Visualise and create the image of a ball of golden energy, or intense white light, building up between your hands. Sense and feel the energy building. Continue to move your hands back and forth, alternately moving them at different speeds: slowly, rapidly and then slowly again. Sense the size of the energy ball and feel the qualities of the energy as much as you possibly can. How big is the ball? How dense is it? What other qualities are you aware of? This exercise will help to increase your awareness of energy.

This technique provides an opportunity to build your confidence and also can be used as a healing technique by placing this ball of energy within the body of a person asking for a healing. Once created in your hands this ball of concentrated healing energy can be physically placed in a person or sent to them long distance through the process of visualisation. Sending healing energy through visualisation is a key element of mind-to-mind and long-distance healing which I will discuss later.

CREATING AN ENERGY CIRCLE/RING — AN EXERCISE

An energy circle or energy ring can be formed to create an energy flow. This can be accomplished with two people, even if neither one has ever had any previous experience of working with energy. Larger numbers of people also can create an energy circle or ring.

For this exercise, I recommend that the participants be sitting comfortably on the floor or in chairs. It is possible to stand, but the process can continue for long periods of time and standing can be tiring.

Each person starts by activating their own energy. Then the left hand is held palm up to receive energy and the right hand is held palm down to send energy. If two people are doing this exercise, they face each other so that each right hand is directly above, but not touching, the partner's left hand.

Choose one person to start the exercise. While the second person holds their hands stationary, the first person raises and lowers their hands, keeping 1-12 inches (2.5-30 cm) of space between the pairs of hands (see Fig. 9). Sense the energy building between your hands and your partner's. How does the energy feel? Move each hand separately, first the right hand and then the left. Is there a difference in the way each hand senses the energy? Allow each person plenty of time to feel the energy. Then reverse roles and allow your partner to raise and lower their hands while you hold your hands still. After sensing the energy, discuss in as

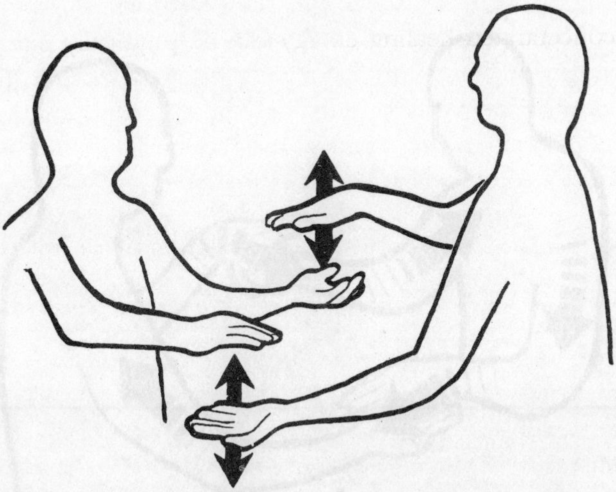

Figure 9 SENSING ENERGY WITH A PARTNER

much detail as possible what each has been feeling. Now go back and do the experiment a second and third time. Feel the energy. Do you have a greater sensitivity and awareness of the energy field? Again, discuss with your partner what it felt like. This discussion with your partner is extremely important because it will open new awarenesses, validate your sensations and assist in bringing to the conscious level sensations that you had but perhaps did not recognise.

Next create a continuous energy circuit by having both partners send energy out from the right hand and receive energy with the left hand (see Fig. 10). This energy loop can be intensified through moving the energy visually. Sense this energy, and see how strong an energy field you can create. Discuss this in detail with each other.

This exercise can also be done with groups of any size. The larger the circle, the greater the potential of the energy field, and the more intense the energy flow can be. Form a circle and sit with your hands extended to the sides, left

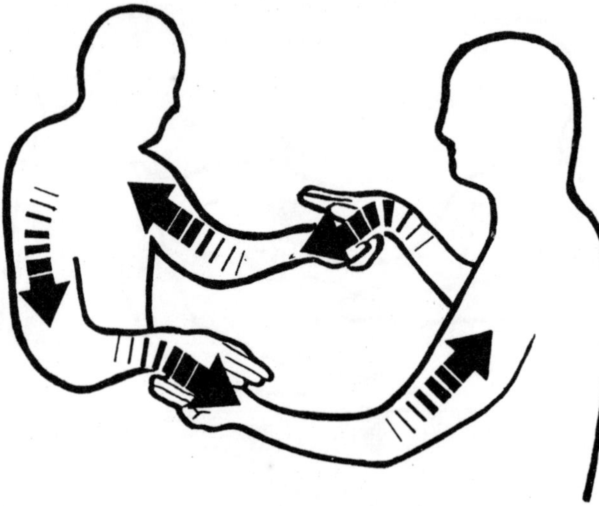

Figure 10 CREATING CONTINUOUS ENERGY LOOP — TWO PEOPLE

hand palm up and right hand palm down. Hold your hands as in the partner exercise: your right hand above your partner's left hand. Send energy to the person on your right and receive energy from the person on your left (see Fig. 11). In this manner the energy flows counter-clockwise around the circle. Visualisation enhances the energy flow and helps the energy to move more easily. As you send energy and visualise its flow increasing, you create an energy field that becomes stronger and stronger as the energy circulates. Most people can feel the movement of energy in their body, as well as the buildup of an energy field in the air around the group. After you sense the energy, you can physically connect with your partners by holding hands. (Maybe this is why good friends and lovers hold hands; they are sharing their energy.) Notice that energy naturally flows from left to right. Always agree on this direction of energy flow ahead of time with whomever you are working,

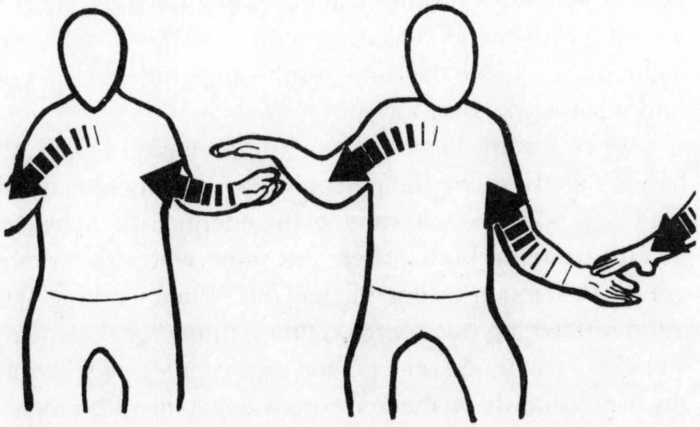

Figure 11 CREATING CONTINUOUS ENERGY LOOP — GROUP

so that everyone visualises energy flowing in the same direction.

After experimenting with sending only energy, add the visualisation of sending a colour such as white, gold, emerald green or pink and sense the differences in the way each colour feels. Discuss what each person has felt and how they experienced it.

Again, the purpose of these exercises is to experience the energy, to learn to feel comfortable with energy and to gain confidence by actually working with it. Energy is always present. It is your friend and is always there to help you. The key is to learn how to use it and to direct its flow.

POSITIONING OF HANDS

The positioning of your hands as well as the way you use them may change from time to time, varying with your sensitivity to energy, the type of healing work you are doing and the person with whom you are working. The way I work with energy is the way that works best for me. Each person who does healing will develop a personal style of working with energy. I have seen many different styles and techniques achieve the same results. Experiment until you find what works best for you.

When I want to sense someone's energy, I hold my hands slightly above the person or very lightly directly on the body. Some people can feel the energy 2-12 inches (5-30 cm) from the body. There are some who can feel the energy field much farther out than this. When working with a tumour, taking out energy, putting in energy, balancing a chakra or working on a person's arms or legs, I will hold my hands directly on the body or I will hold them 2-6 inches (5-15 cm) from the body. In all cases, I proceed according to my sense of what that person needs. When approaching sexual areas or sensitive injured areas it is not appropriate, nor is it important, to be in physical contact with the area. It is just as effective to work 2-6 inches away from the body. With an aura cleansing always keep your hands 2-6 inches away from the body. As each healing is unique, act according to what feels most appropriate at the time.

Most of the time when I am doing healings, especially when I am draining out negative energy or putting in healing energy, I hold my fingers together with my palms facing the person. Energy also can be focused from the finger tips like a laser beam for concentrating and sending energy into a specific area (see Fig. 12). This energy can be used much like a scalpel for doing surgery on internal energy blockages.

When I am doing an aura cleansing, especially if I am working over a wide area, I will keep my fingers together as mentioned above but will hold my thumbs out from my hands. As I work, I position my hands next to each other with my thumbs almost touching. When sweeping the

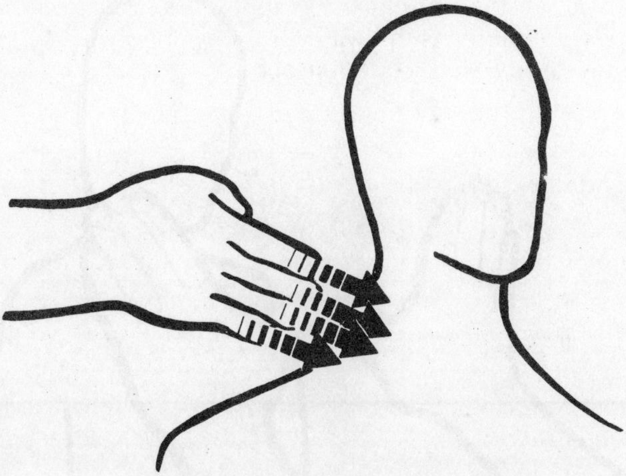

Figure 12 ENERGY FORMING LASER BEAMS

energy field with two hands I keep my hands moving together, using them as one unit (see Fig. 13). This method covers a large area more quickly. When working with a small area, I use one or both hands moving together or independently while visualising that I am smoothing out the energy field, much like smoothing out the icing of a cake.

As I describe specific healing techniques later I will go into greater detail as to hand placement and the distance to hold the hands from the body. These will serve as a reference point for you as you do your own healing work.

HOW TO SENSE ENERGY IN THE BODY

Now that you have experimented with building energy balls and energy rings, you are ready to start sensing the energy in another person's body. Most of the people that I have worked with are able to start sensing energy in another person within a few minutes. Once you are able to feel the energy for the first time, it is very easy to feel

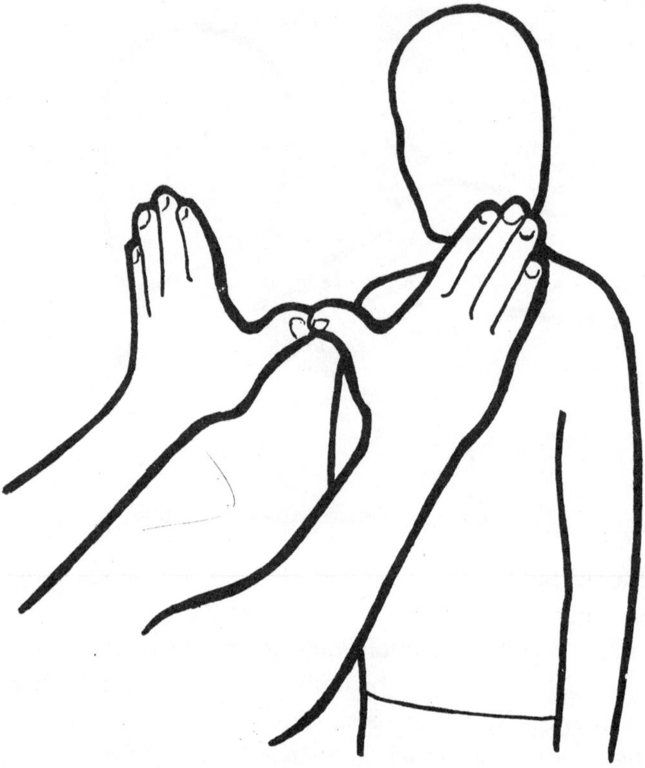

Figure 13 USE OF TWO HANDS FOR AURA CLEANSING

energy again and to build rapidly upon that experience. It is helpful to relax into feeling the energy and not to rush or judge yourself. For most people, sensing energy is an entirely new experience and, as with all new skills, it takes a while to become comfortable with it. Remember to be patient and gentle with yourself. Some people sense energy best with the hand lightly touching the body, while others prefer to hold the hand 1-6 inches (2.5-15 cm) away from the body. Everyone is different. Once you become familiar with feeling another's energy, you can begin working on improving this skill. The ability to sense and feel energy will stay with you always; it can be recalled many years later, even if not actively used in the meantime.

Exercise: Sense energy for yourself

The person being worked with can be in any position for this exercise. However, I prefer to have them lying on their back. To sense energy, hold your hand, palm down, slightly beyond the person's head. Keeping your hand 1-6 inches (2.5-15 cm) above the body, move your hand very slowly down the body from head to feet. As you move your hand, you can usually see, intuit or feel differences in the temperature of various areas of the body. Both excessive heat and cold are indicators that the energy is not flowing openly and evenly, and is out of balance. Heat is an indicator that excess energy is blocked, building up or being released from the body. Heat can also suggest that anger or rage is being held in, or is overflowing from the body. Cold is an indicator that the energy flow is shut down or constricted. A person who is scared for any reason may withdraw and shut down their energy flow. This creates cold spots in their energy field. When a person is very shut down, these cold spots may feel like ice. Cold hands and cold feet can be caused by a person being in trauma or terror. When the fear is released their energy flow opens up and the hands and feet become warm and remain so.

Sensing for hot and cold spots provides indicators as to what is going on in the person with whom you are working. Remember that the temperature differences are relative to the person's overall body temperature. Lack of obvious hot or cold places may mean that the person is fairly well energetically balanced at that moment. It can also mean that the person's issues have not been triggered and therefore the energy reaction has not been activated. To trigger the issues and the emotions, I usually spend at least 5-15 minutes talking to a person about the issues to be worked on.

You will experience many other feelings and sensations

as you become more sensitive to working with energy. Sometimes, when the hands are held over a person or moved over their body, tingling, smoothness or roughness in the energy field can be felt.

Tingling or roughness might be indicators of excess or disrupted energy. Disrupted energy includes breaks in and injury to the energy field around the body, caused by emotional trauma, physical injury or surgery. This can be smoothed out using the aura cleansing technique. Every sensation is an indicator that may assist in pinpointing areas needing attention. Over time you will instinctively develop your own method of sensing energy and of interpreting what you are sensing.

Repeat this exercise using your other hand. Now experiment using both hands at once. Repeat this exercise three or four times. Are you becoming more sensitive to the energy? Are you getting additional sensations as you become more comfortable sensing the energy?

If you are practising with partners in addition to the person lying down, have them sense the energy field also. Then discuss what each of you is feeling and where you are feeling it. Notice what you feel that is similar as well as what feels different. If you are feeling different sensations from your partner, go over the body again focusing on the area in question. Working in partnership can greatly expand your awareness of energy.

NOTE – Even if you and your partner have very different experiences, trust yourself. You may be sensing different levels of the person's energy. Please remember to trust your own process and to allow yourself to sense the energy your own way.

Four

UNDERSTANDING HEALING

HOW MUCH TIME DOES HEALING TAKE?

Healing occurs on many different levels — mental, physical, emotional and spiritual. In most sessions, energy shifts occur within the body which can be recognised by both the healer and the person being worked with. When a noticeable feeling or sensation is experienced within the body, it is much easier for the conscious mind to accept that something has actually happened. In many healings a person will experience an immediate shift in their energy and, usually, a greater sense of well-being and relaxation — an inner peace, an inner knowing, an inner awareness and greater clarity.

A healing session can also release an energy blockage within someone that begins a slow healing process which may continue very gently over a period of days, weeks or even years. This subtle shift might go totally unnoticed at first. In these cases, the individual might not even realise the healing process is occurring or that a shift in their energy field is taking place.

One of the most important lessons I have had to learn is to allow the process to take as much time as it needs. In this result-oriented society it is a challenge to refrain from trying for immediate and identifiable results in the person being worked with. Focusing on and striving for results can actually diminish the quality of the healing session, and can lessen the likelihood of healing. An excellent statement to make at the end of a healing session is to tell the person in a soft, supportive voice to 'take as much time as you need to heal'. In this way, you do not rush or push the person or the energy. This allows the person to feel safer, totally accepted and unconditionally loved. The more comfortable they feel, the more accepted, the less judged and criticised, the faster the healing will occur. Most of the illnesses that people experience are the result of their self-criticism, self-judgement, fear, anger and pain. They perceive that they have been hurt and they shut down to protect themselves. If we, as healers, bring our own judgements and expectations to the healing process, we are actually compounding the 'cause' of the illness in the individual we are working to heal. The gentler we are with ourselves and with other people, the easier, the quicker and the more profound the healings.

In some ways healing is much like baking. Baking depends on certain ingredients, the heat of the oven and the cooking time. Likewise, healing involves a person's issues (the ingredients), the amount of healing energy required (the heat), and the time needed for the healing energy to release the blockage (time). Some of the main ingredients might be related to the mental, physical, emotional or spiritual challenges with which a person is dealing.

The other ingredients might be the readiness and willingness of a person to heal. Some challenges require only a little energy to heal, while others need much more healing energy. The more someone feels guilt, shame and fear and the more their identity is attached to his issues, the more energy and time it will take to heal.

Just as the oven supplies the heat, the healer supplies the healing energy. Different healers are capable of transmitting different amounts and qualities of healing energy.

The time a healing takes might be understood as the actual physical time required to release the negative energy, and replace it with the healing energy. A more technical approach might include the time until the healing has integrated within the person. Here again the amount of energy transmitted, the skill of the healer and the willingness of the person to surrender and heal all play a large part in the time required for healing.

WHY IS HEALING SOMETIMES PAINFUL?

In cases where people have either suppressed their feelings or, consciously or subconsciously, allowed their coping mechanism to help them avoid facing a potentially painful situation, they have not released their pain. When pain occurs and is not acknowledged, experienced or dealt with, it is unresolved and becomes an energy blockage which remains in the body and creates illness.

Sometimes during a healing session the energy within a person's body will start moving, seeking balance and healing, and will open up old, unhealed emotional wounds. Although old emotional wounds are the most common, these wounds might exist on a mental, physical, emotional or spiritual level, or a combination of these. As these old emotional wounds open, a person might experience the pain that they have held inside but were never before consciously aware of. Because it takes a lot of effort to suppress thoughts and feelings, this stored pain has drained energy from the person. Once this pain is released, the old, destructive emotions are also released and the person's energy level usually increases. Tears and sobbing are indications that a person has released an old wound.

It is very important that people allow themselves to feel all of their feelings. Only by surrendering into and feeling the pain and hurt can they move through them.

A friend shared this example with me: He observed his spiritual teacher accidentally step on some floor boards that weren't nailed in place. As he stepped on them, the boards separated and his leg was hurt as it slipped between them. Rather than shutting down to avoid the pain, which most would do, the teacher stayed with it, embraced it and breathed into and through the pain. By feeling the pain and allowing it to be, he was letting it pass through his body and would never have to experience it again. If he had suppressed the pain, he might have locked some of the energy in his body, requiring him to release this energy at a later time.

The following exercise demonstrates how people become used to pain in their bodies — to the point where they do not even feel it. It also shows how the body, as it heals, sometimes experiences pain even though it is obvious that it is healing. This exercise clearly shows that pain is not always an enemy.

Exercise

Hold your arm straight out in front of you. Make a tight fist and squeeze it as hard as you possibly can. You might experience some pain in your hand and arm. Within about 15 seconds however the hand starts to become numb. Continue to hold your fist tightly for another minute or two. Notice that the pain seems to go away completely. Continue to hold your fist tightly clenched for as long as you can. When you absolutely cannot hold it any longer, very slowly and gently start opening your hand. You will feel a lot of pain, especially as your fingers start to stretch out. As long as your fist was tightly closed there didn't seem to be any pain. It was only when the hand was opened and stretched that the pain became pronounced.

This is much like healing. When old patterns are beginning to release, there can be some pain. In reality, the problem began with the tight muscles, the tension — the clenched fist of the exercise. Over time a person can become so accustomed to pain and tension that they are no longer aware of it and accept it as a normal part of life. Examples of this are tense shoulder and back muscles, a knot in the stomach and even headaches.

As children, few if any of us had the skills and psychological tools to take care of ourselves. In order to survive, most of us learned how to compensate rather than to face and heal our issues and illnesses. As adults, we tend to adjust our lifestyle to avoid dealing with our issues rather than clearing these issues and healing our illnesses. The methods described throughout this book will assist in releasing and healing issues at the core level of a person's being.

FACTORS AFFECTING A HEALING

The degree of healing a person receives depends on a combination of factors. These can be broken down into three main categories: (1) the ability of the healer, including the amount and quality of energy the healer can channel; (2) the nature of the illness or the discomfort; and (3) the ability and willingness of the person receiving the healing to let go of the problem and allow themself to be healed.

The first factor is the healer. An effective healer has the skills through spiritual guidance and personal talents to channel and focus healing energy. The healer's intention is to increase the healing energy level sufficiently for healing to occur. Another important quality is the healer's ability to create an environment in which the person being healed feels safe and supported. The healer's skill, such as intuitively knowing what to say to the person being worked with, and when and how, is also extremely important.

The second factor is the severity of the illness. Although it may appear that the nature of an illness is an indication of the potential degree of difficulty in achieving a healing, this has not always been the case in my experience. I personally have experienced people who seemed more resistant to releasing relatively minor ailments such as headaches, stress and fear than did people facing life-threatening illnesses. What I believe to be true is that any and all illnesses can be healed.

The third factor is the readiness and willingness of the

person to receive healing. In both of the total healings described earlier the people involved had done a lot of personal preparation mentally, physically, emotionally and spiritually. The more relaxed, open and willing a person is to be trusting, to feel their feelings, to surrender into their pain and to let go, the easier it is for them to release the energy locked in their body. Yes, the ability of the healer and the amount of energy a healer can channel are important. Yet they are not nearly as important as most would think. The willingness of the person to receive healing energy is far more critical than the healer's ability.

Healing is in some ways much like planting a garden. If you take the time to till the soil, to fertilise it, to water it and to clear out the rocks, you can be fairly confident that the seeds you plant will sprout and produce results. If, however, you just throw seeds on unprepared ground, there is little, if any, chance of the seeds growing.

DEGREES OF HEALING

Healings fall into three general categories: complete healings, partial healings and those with no noticeable results. These categories involve differences in the amount of time it takes for the healing to manifest, the degree of healing achieved, and whether the person can feel a change in their energy level, emotions or physical body.

Complete healings are best divided into two sub-categories: minor and major complete healings. A minor complete healing would include elimination of aches, pains, headaches and minor burns. A major complete healing, often described as a miracle healing, would include healing cancer, high blood pressure, arthritis or a similar ailment. Complete healings of minor ailments are fairly common and are readily achieved even by beginning healers. Major complete healings, where an obvious, complete and dramatic healing occurs instantaneously, are less common. Most complete healings, both minor and major, involve progressive changes which take some time to integrate.

The two major complete healings of serious illness described in this book involve women who had done much personal growth work prior to the healing. Personal growth work includes counselling, bodywork, dietary changes, meditation, reading and prayer. In many ways the process of healing is a process of surrendering old patterns, forgiving or making peace with oneself and others, and accepting one's own self-worth. The more people are open to change and have prepared themselves to receive the gift of healing, the faster, easier and more complete the healing will be.

The second category is by far the most common. Here the person receives a partial healing. Even though the person can readily sense and recognise a definite physical shift and/or notice a difference in the way they are feeling, the healing might not be complete. Some of these people report a high degree of healing, while others report only minimal response or temporary relief.

The third category, representing less than 5% of all those I have worked on, are people who report feeling nothing and who seem to have no readily identifiable shift in their energy, at least during the healing session. In those who did not seem to experience change, I have noticed a number of possible reasons. Most of these people seemed to be emotionally shut down, having been badly traumatised at some time in their life. Fear appears to be the main reason. This includes fear of the unknown or the fear that if they allow themselves to release control of their emotions and be open and vulnerable, even for a short period of time, they will not survive or be safe. Their fear of the unknown and the need to protect themselves is greater than their desire for healing. There are times when a person is in an environment where any change may trigger a life-threatening situation. In this case, change may need to wait until the person can create a safer environment

Surprisingly, many people grow so accustomed to pain that the prospect of a life without pain is not only potentially unsettling, but also frightening. This untested life-without-pain becomes more of a threat than the known quantity of pain that they experience on a daily basis. In fact some people can actually become addicted to their pain. There are many cases of battered women who repeatedly go back to abusive husbands rather than accept the help of friends and others. The idea of change alone can trigger the fear of the unknown, even if it is a change for the better, especially when self-image is poor or self-esteem is low. Please note that even this category might experience a partial or complete healing, which may take time to become evident.

There are other reasons for a person not accepting a healing. Perhaps they are not ready to change or the life lesson involved may not have been learned. The body, the mind and the spirit are much smarter and more aware than people realise. It may not be in the highest and best interest of the person to change at that time.

I estimate that more than 95% of those who receive healing energy actually feel at least some sensations of this energy. Although almost everyone receiving a healing feels different after a session, it might take days before a person becomes consciously aware of the extent of the changes that have taken place. These might include the impact the healing has on their health, as well as changes in the way they relate to and function in their environment. As a healer, I am seldom aware of the full impact the healing energy has on a person's life. Many times, especially if you travel a lot or only see a person a few times, you may not remain in close contact with the people you work with and therefore will not be aware of long-range benefits. It has taken me a long time to trust that, even when I was unable to perceive a shift in a person's energy, a complete healing might have taken place. Because the benefits of a healing may have set in motion a shift that might take days, weeks or even longer to become evident, absolute classification is almost impossible. For example, I worked with two different women, one of whom had a fear of flying and the other had feelings of abandonment because of the death of a parent during early childhood. In both cases I was not able to confirm a healing immediately. After many weeks each woman called to share her amazement that she was now able to do things calmly that in the past triggered her fears and anxieties.

Always ask for feedback on what the person felt during a healing session. If you work on an issue that cannot immediately be verified, ask the person to stay in touch and let you know how they do when confronting a similar situation.

Keeping a journal and/or records about what you try and what happens in your healing sessions, as well as communicating with other healers, can be helpful in discovering approaches to healing that work best for you.

Five

UNDERSTANDING ILLNESS

ILLNESSES AND INJURIES

There are basically two kinds of illness and injury. First there are those illnesses and injuries that seem to be created from outside the body — including accidents, burns and infections, which appear to be activated or stimulated as a result of an external incident.

The second kind stem from people's internal processes of reacting to, or protecting themselves from, external events. These reactions can include anger, fear, insecurity, judgement and hurt and they may be directed toward the self or others. Intense emotions are the result of energy locked in the body. Unless our reactions are acknowledged and resolved, they create and stimulate many of the physical ailments that plague us, including cancer, heart problems and high blood pressure.

NOTE: Many believe, as I do, that even seemingly externally-caused illnesses and injuries are created by a subconscious desire to hurt or punish ourselves or by the superconscious/higher self trying to grab our attention and help us learn something. The healing techniques described in this book will work regardless of the perceived source of the illness or injury.

PAIN AND ILLNESS AS A GIFT

Traditionally Western culture views both pain and illness as negative and destructive. In reality, pain and illness may be viewed as great gifts because they are signs that the body is out of balance and is crying out for help. Every time we experience pain or illness, our body is trying to communicate something. All pain and illness are directly connected to energy blockages and, taking this one step further, all energy blockages are caused by being in disharmony — we are out of alignment within ourselves in some way.

By observing what is occurring in the body and where it is occurring we can gain valuable insights into what is causing imbalance in our life. (See 'How the Body Communicates' at the end of this book.) When we listen to our body and help correct its imbalances, we not only heal very quickly, but we also improve the overall quality of our life.

ROOT CAUSE OR CORE-LEVEL ISSUES

Most people, in order to cope with everyday life, have taken on an identity, a persona, which they present to the world so they will be loved and accepted. These false fronts assist in hiding and protecting true feelings, thoughts, ideas and values from the world. They are masks that hide sensitivity and vulnerability. Examples include: a person who is in extreme pain but wears a happy face so as not to disappoint others, a soldier who detests violence but who forces himself to remain in the military, a caregiver who is burnt out but keeps smiling and giving because it is all they know how to do, or possibly someone who is gay yet is pretending to be straight. Once these false fronts are put on, it requires tremendous courage to take them off again.

When someone is wearing a mask, many issues that they appear to be dealing or coping with successfully are in reality festering time bombs.

Almost all issues, symptoms and illnesses are the exposed surface of much deeper hidden issues. Healing the surface symptoms has only a minimal effect until the core issue, the root cause of the challenge, is addressed.

For example, cancer or another life-threatening illness might appear on the surface to be the cause of many negative effects in the body. However, if we go deeper we will most likely discover that the cancer actually is an effect of the festering poison of anger, resentment or a feeling of futility.

If we can get in touch with, shift and heal the deepest level of our issues, the healing that occurs is more profound.

Core-level issues develop from traumatic experiences, such as rape, incest, abandonment, betrayal or any event that has had a significant negative impact on us. When initially confronted with these traumas, we either did not have the skills or were too young or unable to take care of ourselves. As a result, we shut down to avoid being hurt and thereby trapped the physical pain and emotional trauma in our body. This negative energy then became locked in our body and our auric field, causing us to become less than who we are. As this energy is released and the underlying issues heal, we can begin to live a more normal life and deal more effectively with everyday experiences.

Some common core-level issues and decisions that undermine our lives are:

"Who I am is not okay"
"I'm never enough"
"I'm not lovable"
"I can never do it right"
"If they find out who I really am, they won't love me"

Core-level issues involve deep trauma as well as shame, guilt, fear and grief.

When working with a person, constantly ask yourself and the person, "Is there a deeper issue here?" "What is behind these feelings?" "When did you decide to get sick?" You can even ask the taboo questions, "When did you decide to die?" and "Why did you decide to die?" These questions, when asked with love, compassion, an open heart and a soft, gentle voice, might help a person to open to a deep awareness and to an equally deep emotional release.

Sometimes it is important to work with the surface issues first, because this provides a safe place to begin the healing process. As a level of trust is built between the healer and the individual, deeper issues may be addressed. Once a core-level issue is addressed, resolved and healed, a major transformation can occur without effort. It is when these core-level issues are healed that dramatic changes in a person's life and interaction patterns occur.

THOUGHT FORMS

Thought forms are ideas, concepts or fears, created by the self or others, that we have accepted on some level as being true. These thought forms can be detected in the auric field; they are ever-present in both the mind and the energy field, affecting every moment of life. Thought forms can be either positive or negative, depending upon whether or not they contribute to our overall well-being. Negative thought forms can be cleared from the auric field through aura cleansings.

In 1981 a very psychic psychologist named Jill told me that my father was planning to die from an illness within the next few years. At that time my father, who lived over 1500 miles away, seemed to be in perfect health and had no outward signs of illness. In March of 1983 he died of cancer and emphysema at age 63. Jill had tuned in to the thought form created by my father's decision to die.

A thought form frequently can be detected in the energy field from three months to five years before an actual illness manifests in the physical body. In my opinion, these thoughts or decisions that are held in the body's energy field might come from a person's conscious or unconscious desire to give up, or to punish, destroy, hurt or even kill themself. These negative thoughts first show up as small clouds or pinpoints of dark energies in the outer reaches of the energy field. Then slowly, over time, they grow — becoming larger and more dense, moving closer and closer to the physical body until eventually the cells in the body manifest an illness.

Thought forms can be positive and uplifting or negative and draining. Positive thought forms are created through positive prayer, affirmations and the visualisation of positive outcomes. If a person chooses to stop destroying themself, decides to change negative feelings and belittling self-talk and chooses to heal, the destructive process can be halted and even reversed. I have seen people heal very quickly once they faced their challenges and made a clear decision to heal.

When working with people with life-threatening illnesses, a healer can sometimes help a person to make a dramatic breakthrough by asking such direct questions as "What in your life can't you face?" "What in your life can't you change?" "What in your life can't you forgive yourself for?" "What in your life can't you forgive someone else for?" What you are searching for by asking these questions is the erroneous decision this person has made about their life. This decision causes feelings of futility, being boxed in or having no power over their life. The questions are aimed at triggering awareness of the negative thought pattern or the core level issue behind an illness. With this awareness comes the pivotal point at which the person can choose either to face the issue and live or to avoid the issue and die.

I have heard of a medical doctor who works only with cases that other doctors have classified as 'terminal'. By talking with his patients and asking them what in their lives they cannot face or change, by listening with an open heart to their stories and by helping them to see that they do have options, he has helped more than 70% of them to survive and heal.

Through personal experience and the experiences related by many other healers, I know that illnesses — even those classified as terminal — can be healed once a turnaround in attitude has occurred.

Releasing negative thought forms can be achieved through aura cleansings, using positive thoughts (affirmations) and working with healing energy to clear both the body and the energy field. This is vitally important to maintaining good health on all levels.

HIERARCHY OF PAIN AND PROTECTION

Few of us were raised in a family that was consistently nurturing and supportive, providing us with unconditional love. All of us, to varying degrees, have suffered physical, emotional, mental and spiritual anguish as a result of our childhood and life experiences.

We all have experienced pain, trauma and disappointment. Some of us have been able to handle it better than others. As pain or disappointment increases in intensity, it becomes hurt, anger, rage and sometimes even terror. As the intensity of the pain and abuse increases, it becomes exceedingly difficult to stay open and loving, regardless of how much we might want to. At some point, we are forced to choose between confronting our abusers and stopping the abuse or shutting down to protect ourselves, running away, going insane or dying. Few children growing up in homes where they experience trauma are able to confront and change their abusers or run away. Most learn to shut down at least some of their feelings in order to survive.

People take care of themselves as best they can. When faced with intense pain, ongoing stress or a sudden shock we might, without even being consciously aware of what we are doing, shut down to protect ourselves. We might go into a state of shutdown when confronted with situations or issues in our life that we refuse to see, feel or deal with, or when an experience is either too painful or too shocking to tolerate.

Anything overwhelming might cause us to shut down. Some examples include the death of a parent, brother, sister or even a pet, especially if this occurred when we were very young. Other situations include moving to a new location, an accident, being sexually abused or being around someone who, in anger or rage, might be verbally or physically abusive. Any form of physical, emotional, mental or spiritual abuse can create feelings of shock, trauma, panic or abandonment, triggering a partial or complete shutdown.

This shutting down process is an automatic, instinctive survival mechanism of the body in order to avoid pain and to maintain the illusion of being in control. This survival mechanism is at least as strong as the more familiar 'fight or flight' mechanism. Unfortunately, this kind of protection also locks the negative energy into the body and literally can leave a person emotionally crippled at the age of the shutdown.

Some people have blocked out their inner sight and cannot visualise pictures or colours. This could be a form of shutting down and refusing to see the past because it was too painful for them. Others shut down their feelings and either do not feel their bodies or stay in their heads, intellectualising everything almost all the time. People who are shut down might have a tendency to avoid or run from opportunities to work through their issues or may not even be aware that an issue exists.

Examples of people who are most likely to shut down include war veterans who have experienced tremendous trauma during battle (post traumatic stress syndrome), adult children of alcoholics, victims of violent crime, victims of sexual and emotional abuse, battered spouses, people who grew up in a very dysfunctional family and stressed-out business executives. Although the situations are different, the procedure for working with these people is almost identical.

The following Hierarchy of Pain and Protection chart came to me one day while I was helping some people to understand how their previous experiences were connected to their present ones. The chart shows in a graphic way how earlier events affect our lives and how our past experiences create our current challenges.

Shut down/numb/no emotions expressed — energy stuck/frozen

— emotional barrier —

intensity of pain (↑)		
	rage	— energy moving
	anger	
	hurt	
	disappointment	
	conditional love	
	neutral	
	unconditional love	

If a person is in touch with their feelings, it is relatively easy to assist with the healing process. In situations where someone has partially or totally shut down, the work of the healer is much more challenging.

It takes a lot of energy to remain shut down. The person might feel depression or fatigue or be numb to life. They might also have employed the use of food, drugs, alcohol, anger, overwork, violence or sex to mask or suppress their true feelings.

Whenever an individual has been closed down or numb in an area for a long time, they have stored up a lot of emotions. A person who is shut down has a tremendous lid on their feelings and will not allow their true emotions to surface. This total control can be effective for short periods of time, but as the pressure builds and/or the person starts to relax and open up, even a little, this lid begins to crack. As this happens, the uncontrolled emotions might erupt with an intensity that is out of proportion to the current situation that seems to have triggered them. This kind of release tends to frighten both the person experiencing these intense emotions and everyone around them. Unfortunately, the first instinct is to shut down again, or at least to try to, so that they maintain some semblance of control.

The secret of healing is to encourage the person to feel as much of their pain, anger and other suppressed emotions as they can. The more support the person is willing to receive from a healer while going through this healing process, the easier the process will be. Many times people have cried — sometimes hysterically — for long periods of time after coming out of shutdown and experiencing their feelings. Once this barrier has been penetrated and removed, the possibility for tremendous healing and change exists.

SHUT DOWN — STUCK IN TIME

Over time, I have noticed that people who have experienced trauma, especially at a very young age, are emotionally stuck at the age of that trauma. These adults sometimes talk in a little child's voice and seem emotionally frozen in time. They appear to function normally, except that when they are under pressure their responses become childish and irrational. A key indicator of childhood trauma is the inability to function in a way that is consistent with their current age level. This inability to function can be caused by insecurity, immaturity or fear.

This does not mean that the person is immature or

non-functional in all areas of their life. They may, in fact, hold an important position in business or government and function very well in this role. Their personal life, their home life or their sex life might, however, be considerably impaired. An example of this is the workaholic boss who is very successful in business, focusing all of their time and energy on work and avoiding — as much as possible — dealing with personal relationships or social interactions. This person is frequently lonely and uptight, and will have a tendency to develop illnesses as a result of their life being out of balance.

Another example of someone stuck in time is a person who was abused as a child and has made the decision to be a super-pleaser in order to gain some degree of safety through love and acceptance. Frequently this person will talk and act in a childlike way and will go out of their way to assist and support others while putting their own needs aside. Their acts of kindness appear totally selfless and often they are sought after as a friend and business associate. As time goes by they will often burn out because they have over-committed and not taken care of themself. This burn-out can take various forms including exhaustion, illness, blow ups and forgetfulness. As this person heals their abuse issues, they lose their need to please everyone else and start to find out what pleases them. They learn to say 'no' to people and to set appropriate limits and boundaries.

Someone who was emotionally, physically or sexually abused as a child may fall apart when having to confront a superior or other authority figure. Intimate relationships may also be difficult or impossible until the core issues are worked through. As the person faces, clears and heals the trauma, their voice pattern and interaction patterns start to change and will continue to change until stabilising at the maturity level of their current age. This healing will affect the person on all levels — mental, emotional, physical and spiritual.

DENIAL

Denial is the refusal to admit to the validity, existence or significance of a feeling, behaviour or experience which in reality does exist and has a great deal of bearing on our life. Denial can be divided into two types.

The first is the denial of a current behaviour pattern. A perfect example of this kind of denial is the way most substance abusers and other participants in compulsive habits will refuse to admit that their lives are out of control, even when they are acting out their addiction every day.

Most of the time it is not until a person has almost destroyed their life and has 'bottomed out' that they recognise and are willing to admit they have a problem. Only when the denial is broken are they able actively to seek and accept help and begin to heal. Many times, such a person has destroyed everything meaningful in their life before they reach this point of total despair.

The second kind of denial is the denial of a past experience which is too painful, too traumatic or too overwhelming for the conscious mind to accept and integrate. Denial can be considered the fight or flight mechanism of mental survival. This is a natural, human response to any experience or information which, if accepted, could threaten our perception of reality. Denial enables us to function in life more or less as if nothing had happened. Many times it is the denial of trauma that leads to compulsive behaviour and substance abuse to numb the pain.

Whenever we deny a feeling, behaviour or thought, we suppress and stuff the energy associated with it into the body, creating an energy blockage. Denial can deaden the spirit and rob us of our spontaneity and aliveness.

It is common for a victim of childhood sexual abuse to be in denial and to block out memories of sexual advances or violations, especially if these violations came from their parents or caretakers. To hold on to the illusion that their parents love them and support them in a healthy way, the child will deny that the experience ever occurred. Often children stay in denial for years in order to keep loving their parents, to be able to live in the same house as their abusers and to remain sane.

Like all other forms of suppression, denial is not foolproof. With time and stimulus the memories fester like infected cuts and indicators of the denied abuse begin to surface in a person's life. Possible indicators of denied sexual abuse are: crying or recoiling when touched, panicking when someone gets close, avoiding sexual contact and/or feeling shame about lovemaking. The person might also go to the opposite extreme and be promiscuous, becoming sexually out of control. In either case a person might have dreams or flashbacks which bring the memories out little by little.

In general, unresolved traumatic experiences affect almost every aspect of a person's life, hindering their ability to work with others, to trust, to date, to marry and to experience intimacy, until the blockage is cleared. Once the memories are recalled and the denial is broken, the healing process can begin.

Some of these memories may be painful. Although the natural tendency is to suppress emotions to avoid pain, always encourage the person to do exactly the opposite. Encourage them to surrender to their pain, to feel all of their feelings and to experience all of their trauma (or as much as they can deal with at the moment). As they do so, their frozen emotions and memories will be thawed, felt and released. After the release comes a rebuilding period when their self-image and self-esteem must be strengthened. Even after a healing, it takes time to adjust to the new energy and to rediscover, repattern and reprogram the mind, body and emotions in a positive way.

Breaking denial requires an incredible amount of courage and commitment from both the person and the healer. Usually denial is not faced until a situation is so painful that the denial is no longer strong enough to suppress and hide the underlying trauma or emotions. If a person in denial is approached or confronted too strongly they might become scared and retreat even deeper into their denial. Unless the person is totally committed to their breakthrough, I recommend the use of probing questions.

To assist someone in breaking denial, ask them to go deeper into their feelings and to experience them. Ask them if they have any memory of an earlier event similar to the one that triggered their current pain. Encourage them to feel where in their body they are experiencing the pain or tension and then to ask the body what the memory is.

To one degree or another, all people are in denial. Some people deny their abusive childhood, some deny their addictions, some deny that they have any relationship problems and others deny that they have any areas in their lives that require healing. The less people deny the truth about themselves and the people they interact with, the more freely their energy will flow and the healthier they will be. As people break through their denial and work through their issues, they naturally reach a higher level of personal integrity, freeing themselves to act more spontaneously and with increased aliveness.

CONFUSION

In my experience, there are only two distinct causes of confusion. Although the causes are very different, the experience might feel the same in both cases. In the first, people use confusion, either consciously or unconsciously, as an excuse or hide behind it to avoid making decisions and taking action. Here, people are unwilling to take responsibility for themselves and are giving away their power. They remain in confusion and never seem to have enough clarity or support to make a decision and take action, regardless of the quality and quantity of options and suggestions offered, and the amount of support and encouragement given. Confusion is used as a strategy for protection. By staying in chronic confusion and not taking action, people can avoid making a wrong decision and never have to risk upsetting or disappointing anyone. This type of behaviour is typical of children raised in an abusive home where disagreement with authority or having one's own thoughts would cause disapproval, beatings or other punishment. Sometimes even agreeing with the abuser would bring punishment. Statements such as "I don't care," "I don't know" or "It doesn't matter to me", if used frequently, are clues that a person might be protecting himself or herself behind confusion.

In my experience, most of the people who demonstrate this type of behaviour were, as children, highly controlled and abused by their parents or other authority figures. They weren't allowed to develop their own healthy sense of identity. To remain safe in an abusive or volatile household, they learned to give away their identity and power and to become invisible so that they would not trigger, challenge or threaten their abusers. They became expert at playing the 'victim' role. For example, one friend of mine, an adult with two children of her own, could not even decide what flavour ice cream she wanted. Her decision-making ability in many areas of her life was poor and if confronted she was quick to give up her position. Upon being questioned about her past, she shared with me how her father would beat her older brother without apparent warning or provocation. She had learned very early in life that to have strong feelings or opinions was extremely dangerous in her family system. Her confusion to some degree kept her safe. By remaining confused, people relinquish power over their own lives in exchange for some imagined degree of safety.

Once a person realises that they are using confusion as a strategy to avoid making decisions, chooses to stop being confused and starts to face the underlying issues, they automatically begin to release their blocked energy. The healing is now well under way.

In the second type of confusion, the individual is in their power and taking full responsibility for their life. In this case the confusion is only temporary in nature and occurs because the individual is breaking out of old habit patterns or comfort zones into new and uncharted territory where previous reference points and ways of responding to the environment are no longer applicable. As a person releases old behaviours, new ones are not immediately formed. It takes time to find and integrate new references. During this transition time, when old patterns have been released and new references are not yet firmly in place, the mind and the body experience disorientation and confusion. Confusion, in this case, is helpful, productive and the prelude to new levels of clarity. It has been said that confusion is the state before clarity.

In working with confusion it is important first to determine the causes of the confusion. If someone is experiencing confusion to avoid making a decision, the healing might involve a long, slow process during which the person requires the experience of safety and support. As they feel safer they can gingerly take one step at a time, gaining experience and more courage with each step. An American movie entitled 'What about Bob' is a comedy about taking baby steps to conquer fears.

If a person has just made a breakthrough and is on new ground, explaining to them the reason for this confusion is usually enough to provide the initial support they need. Do your best to validate that the breakthrough did occur, and encourage them to be gentle with themself and to take as much time as needed.

Six

The Mind and the Healing Process

HOW THE MIND FUNCTIONS

The mind consists of three main aspects: the conscious, the subconscious and the superconscious.

The conscious mind is the gatekeeper that creates and contains all our attitudes and belief systems and is responsible for reviewing and classifying everything we experience. It makes distinctions, interprets, reasons, limits, rationalises, edits and filters all of the information that comes before it. The conscious mind also restricts, judges, compares, computes and then accepts or rejects information as being valid or not. It is responsible for and insures survival, protecting us from being overwhelmed with negative or false data by making judgements based upon previous information it has already accepted as fact. Every thought, feeling, idea, sensation and experience is filtered through the conscious mind.

The conscious mind operates by accepting the input it agrees with and that fits into its already-operating model. It discriminates against and will delete, reject, ignore or deny any information that does not fit into this established perception. Because the conscious mind creates and contains all of our judgements, it also interprets and governs all of our feelings and emotions. It assigns the emotional charge, positive or negative, to all life experiences. It is the interpreter of all of our life data as it is recalled from the subconscious.

When it functions with accurate information, the conscious mind acts as our guardian and protector. However, it can also be our greatest hindrance to healing and positive change, especially if during early childhood it was fed with negative, incorrect or distorted data. Unfortunately, the conscious mind, because of faulty beliefs, has the ability to deny obvious facts and might delete information vital to the healing process. It is also able to resist or reject change, regardless of how positive an impact the new information or change will have on our life. Remember, the conscious mind uses past experiences as its reference point.

Fortunately the conscious mind can accept new beliefs. Just as it originally established values based upon frightening or traumatic experiences and distorted information, it can now be provided with new, accurate information and supportive experiences. This can be achieved through positive self-talk such as encouraging and affirming the self, unconditionally accepting the self and acknowledging the positive changes being made. The more we communicate with our conscious mind and provide it with positive information, the easier it will be for the healing process to occur. Please note that this is why it is extremely important to point out a positive change whenever it occurs within a person. Confirming energy shifts and releases during a healing session provides reinforcement for the conscious mind that indeed a positive change has occurred.

The subconscious mind operates like a video tape that contains the pure data of every instant of our life. It accepts all information without judgement or emotional charge and is capable of total recall. On this tape are recorded all of the colours, tastes, smells, sounds, sensations and visuals of every event we have ever experienced. (In some cases, especially with the use of guided imagery or hypnotic regression, people can even remember events that occurred in other lifetimes or while they were in the womb.) The subconscious mind stores no emotions, so the emotional charge is missing from this tape until the conscious mind places judgement on the experience. Through visual imagery and guided meditation this video tape can be played back, reviewed, replayed and then — with the guidance of a skilled healer — these reactions and emotions can be healed and permanently reprogrammed through understanding, acceptance and forgiveness.

Once the subconscious is accessed, changes in how a person views their past can occur fairly quickly and easily. Such changes will greatly affect how they feel about life in the present. The key to accessing memories in the subconscious is either to get permission and assistance from the gatekeeper, the conscious mind, or to be skilled enough to bypass this gatekeeper.

The superconscious mind is what I call the God mind. This is the part of us that is connected directly to God, the universal life force energy. Through the superconscious all the information and knowledge of the universe is readily available.

Prayers are answered from the superconscious and the improbable becomes manifested reality. Prayer, visualisation and meditation can help access this wonderful, limitless power.

The healing techniques described in this book utilise all three aspects of the mind. When all three work together it is easier for a complete healing to occur.

Lemon Exercise

One vivid example of how the subconscious and the conscious minds interact is demonstrated by the lemon exercise. Everyone has a memory of tasting a lemon. Although the memory of this experience has been stored in the subconscious, we do not continuously recall this event and taste the lemon in our mouth all the time. If, however, I asked you to recall a time when you bit into a lemon and to remember that distinct sour taste, you would probably start to salivate. (My mouth is salivating as I am writing this!) If I went even further and asked you to close your eyes and experience chewing a piece of lemon, tasting the sharp, sour tang of the lemon juice in your mouth, you could probably taste it almost as well as you would with a real lemon. Simply talking about the experience brings the memory, inactive in the subconscious, into the conscious mind where it is re-experienced. It is this ability that, once understood, can be used to assist people in their healing process.

Another powerful example of how the conscious and subconscious minds work together occurred in 1972. I met someone who was skilled at putting people into a state of deep relaxation. He asked if I would be willing to assist him in an experiment and I agreed. He proceeded to talk to me, having me relax deeply. Then he touched my legs lightly with his hands and told me that this would be what I would feel while he was working with me. He then began patting me rigorously with his hands and telling me that I was a bar of steel. At this point, two people picked me up and suspended me, face up, horizontally between two chairs. My head was resting on one of the chairs while the heels of my shoes were resting on the other, with no support underneath me. A moment later I felt what I perceived to be a pair of hands lightly touching my thighs, exactly as before. Being totally conscious and aware of what was going on, I waited a moment or so and then became curious and opened my eyes. I was shocked to see a slim woman about 5 feet 4 inches and 115 pounds standing on me unassisted, with one foot on each of my thighs. Immediately my conscious mind took over — rejecting the possibility of what I was seeing — and I collapsed, unable to hold her any longer. I had no foundation for integrating the reality of the experience and so my conscious mind could not believe it. Since then, I have walked on hot coals, bent six-foot lengths of 3/8-inch rebar steel using my throat and tapped much more strongly into the power of my subconscious and superconscious.

Authority figures, parents and other people in powerful

positions must be aware of their ability to bypass the critical nature of the conscious mind and to enter unhampered directly into a person's subconscious. When this is done, whether for the person's benefit or not, most people will respond by going along with the authority figure's suggestion — usually without even understanding why.

The power of the subconscious mind to accept suggestions, especially when the information is coming from an accepted authority figure, explains why and how placebos work. An individual's susceptibility and vulnerability to suggestions reveals the critical importance of words, whether they are directed toward another or are thoughts and self-talk directed at the self.

Doctors and nurses know that a few key sentences spoken in an operating or recovering room, such as: "The operation was very successful," "You are doing extremely well," "You are stronger even than we imagined," "The operation wasn't as serious as we thought it would be," "You are healing very quickly," can speed the recovery process.

This understanding of the awesome power of the conscious and subconscious encourages the use of every positive means available to reprogram and repattern this great computer system we call the mind.

ATTITUDES AND BELIEF SYSTEMS

Attitudes and belief systems are stored in the conscious mind and form the very foundations of our thinking. They are the filters through which we see and interpret our life and the world. A dozen people can observe a specific incident and each will describe the experience differently according to their individual attitudes and beliefs.

In 1982 I visited my father for the last time before he died. During the visit he told me, "Michael, I finally figured out what our problem has been all these years. It's as simple as the difference between the words 'stubborn' and 'determined'. Your actions are totally immaterial, it's all in the way 'I' feel about them. If I agree with what you are doing, you're 'determined'. If I disagree with what you are doing, then you're 'stubborn'!" My father's statement clearly reflects what a powerful impact our attitude and belief systems can have on our lives.

Core attitudes and beliefs constitute the most sacred laws of how we view ourself and our world and form the basis of our self-image and self-esteem. If these are askew or incorrect, we act in accordance with the defective law rather than live with the truth. Regardless of the amount of information available to contradict this defective law, we will continue to act in alignment with it until we heal the experience that caused the erroneous belief in the first place. A core belief that we must work hard for something to be worthwhile can rob us of gifts and friendships that come to us easily. A belief that 'I am not good enough' will cause us to sabotage success in our life and to discount positive recognition, regardless of how many indications we have that others care about us.

Insecurity can lead us to believe that we need to have more and more to be okay. We all know of people who have accumulated vast sums of money and yet do not feel either secure or safe. Obviously their internal insecurity is not healed by outer materialism. It is the internal attitude and belief that holds them in bondage. And what about the person who believes that they are overweight and tries dieting, even though by medical standards they are already below their recommended weight? Here again it is their perception, attitudes and beliefs that are tormenting them.

As we change our attitudes and belief systems, the quality of our life changes dramatically. A client who is a corporate executive was very suspicious of the healing work that I do. As a child he was raised in a very conservative, superstitious family and was plagued by fears of doing evil and going to hell. Because of these fears he was very hesitant to allow me to assist him. Due to the pain that he was in and because of the trust he had in me as an individual, he finally allowed me to work with him. As we unravelled his past and dealt with his fears, he was able to make a great change in his perception of life and God. As a result of the emotional release he experienced, his blood pressure dropped from 200/120 to 160/94 and his doctor took him off the medication he had been taking. This represented an important shift in his attitudes and belief systems, which created major changes in his life in general.

The way that various Native American tribes perceive the owl is another example of how different our attitudes can be and how they affect people. In some Native American tribes the owl is welcomed and honoured as a sacred bird, almost as much as the eagle; while in other tribes it is feared and considered the harbinger of death. My understanding is that the fear of the owl is so strong in some tribes that if an owl flies into a tepee the owner will burn it down without removing any possessions. The owl is the same bird in both cases; only the attitudes and belief systems of the various tribes are different.

From the moment we reach a state of consciousness in the womb, we begin to form our attitudes and belief systems. The conscious mind is constantly looking for ways to avoid pain and to help us survive. In this process the mind makes fundamental decisions about the nature of reality. Even after we recognise that many of these decisions are not in our best interest, it takes focus and commitment to reprogram and repattern our behaviour. The reprogramming of a major behaviour pattern is rarely instantaneous.

If a person's mother was traumatised while pregnant with them, they might develop an attitude, even at this early stage, that the world is not a safe place. As they grow up they might develop a personality that automatically shuts down, and is closed, defensive, insecure and nervous.

If a person was raised in a family where money was

scarce and the basic necessities were lacking, as was the case for many people who experienced the Great Depression, they might grow up to be very frugal and conservative or they might go to the opposite end of the spectrum and become extremely free with their money. Either reaction is out of balance and can lead to compulsive or obsessive behaviour.

RESTRUCTURING AND REPATTERNING

Humans are creatures of habit and habits are created over time. Because we have learned to live with old habit patterns and have become accustomed to them, we might want to stay with them even after we have broken their hold on us, rather than move forward with the healing process. When we break an old habit pattern or clear an energy block, we create an opportunity for change. Change, combined with the responsibilities that go with it, might have a tendency to bring up fear. It is this fear and the responsibilities incurred in changing that we must face if we are to heal.

A vivid example that illustrates the importance of repatterning and reprogramming is the story of how baby elephants are trained. Once trained, they are fairly easily controlled for the rest of their lives.

When an elephant is a baby, a strong chain is fastened around its leg and then secured to a sturdy object. At first the baby elephant struggles long and hard against the chain. In time, finally realising and accepting that it cannot get away, the baby elephant surrenders to the chain, giving up its struggle to free itself. It learns at this young age that once the chain is attached it cannot get away and hence becomes docile. The elephant has made the association of 'chain on leg . . . can't get away . . . struggle useless . . . surrender' and from this time on the elephant, once chained, remains docile unless severely provoked.

As the elephant grows larger and stronger, there comes a time when it could easily break the chain and become free. The chain is not strong enough to imprison the elephant at this point. Only the old habits and programming of the young elephant are holding it captive now.

Note that the only physical event or physical stimulation is the attachment of the chain. All the other associations are thoughts or decisions made in the elephant's mind. Once upon a time when the elephant was small, this sequence was valid. Now, with the elephant larger and more powerful, the association is no longer valid, yet it still holds the elephant in bondage.

People are much the same. They are held captive by old chains — their attitudes and belief systems and negative patterns and programming — even though as adults they are more than strong enough to confront and break these bonds.

Many sources say that if a person practises new patterns, using techniques like affirmations and new behaviours, for as few as 21 days, these changes become positive habits. Once accepted into the mind any thought, idea or association becomes more difficult to change, as is evident with the elephant. The longer a person holds a thought and the more strongly they believe it or the more they are attached to it, the more fiercely they defend it from change!

Once a person's chains are removed, repatterning and reprogramming with new attitudes and beliefs is extremely important to prevent the person from falling back into the same old rut. This is why it is critical for people going through change to have support from friends, groups or organisations and to be involved in ongoing activities which further encourage, promote and support positive change.

RITUALS

For many years I did not believe in rituals. One day I realised that rituals are simply a way to bring people together. They provide individuals with both a structure for interacting and a road map to help them move from point A to point B on their spiritual paths. Rituals can involve church, government or any other group and may represent times of celebration, prayer, initiation or turning points in life. If we did not have formal rituals to attend which bring us together — like church services, holiday gatherings, weddings, funerals, sweat lodge ceremonies and Indian pipe ceremonies — many of us would tend to isolate ourselves.

Rituals tend to have a structure that provides everyone, especially those new to a group, with a feeling of reassurance and safety. After attending for a few times, people generally become comfortable with most rituals and are willing to take an active part in them. They tend to give people a sense of belonging and a group identity. Humans are creatures of habit and like the security of knowing what is going to happen next. Rituals may provide the elements of safety and structure people don't have anywhere else in their lives.

A ritual is also a roadmap that can lead to a spiritual experience. Once an individual, or a group, has had a peak experience, it is human nature to want to share it with others. After a short period of time, however, many of those leading or experiencing the ritual might begin to believe that it is the only way to acquire that spiritual experience. In time rituals can lose their original meaning and they become increasingly rigid and totally empty of their true spiritual intent.

An example is the story of a famous Guru who placed his cat in a straw basket to protect it from getting trampled during a certain ritual. After the Guru's death his followers would catch a stray cat and put it into a basket, believing it was an important part of the ritual. They had completely forgotten the original purpose of the Guru's action. The original intent of many of the rituals now observed have been lost, changed, added to or diluted. Many of the seemingly meaningless rituals that people participate in today were originally based on teachings which had tremendous value; unfortunately the memory of these teachings has been lost over time.

Spiritual gifts are available without great sacrifice. Among these is spiritual healing. Rituals can be beneficial when they help people align their energy within themselves, and help them open to receiving, forgiving themselves and others, and freeing themselves to see their own goodness. There are many roads to the top of the mountain called spiritual enlightenment. My concern about rituals is that people tend to get caught in the dogma and doctrine and forget the process. The less dogma and doctrine people have to deal with, the purer the message and the lighter the load they carry along the path.

CREATIVE INTENTION

Creative intention is one of the most powerful forces in the universe. It is the desire and commitment to consciously create a specific outcome or event. The mind has the power to create physical reality. The only options we have are (1) to allow the mind to create randomly without discipline or (2) to focus the mind to create our desires. The more we discipline our mind to focus on the positive, the more positive our outcomes will be.

Setting creative intention in motion is like setting the tracking mechanism of a guided missile. Even after launching, the tracking mechanism continues to make course corrections, guiding the missile precisely to its target. Creative intention continues to create and make automatic course corrections long after the initial positive image is conceived, without any conscious effort on our part. Once thought with passion, desire and emotion — whether expressed or not — creative intention sets in motion a powerful energy which can be directed outward for various purposes, such as to send healing energy to someone. It can also be used to attract and magnetise things to us. Creative intention is an extremely powerful tool, whether used for assisting a healing or fulfilling life-long desires or aspirations.

Once we focus our mind on a particular desire, we set in motion tremendous forces. Creative intention aligns the conscious, subconscious and superconscious aspects of the mind, and can create instantaneous healings and other manifestations. The healings of Bonnie and Eagle Feather are perfect examples of how effective creative intention is.

I can remember many incidents when I thought of someone or something and said to myself, "I wonder how ____ is doing?" or "Gee, I wish I had _____," and the person or item I was asking about appeared. Once while out camping, I had a splinter which I couldn't get out and thought, "Gee, I wish I had a pin." Within an hour I found one lying on the ground.

Before starting to write this book I told the universe that I couldn't do it alone and asked for a sign to show me if the universe and Spirit supported this project. I set creative intention into action. Within a few weeks a close friend offered to do the typing, another friend offered me a very nice computer system to use at my home and an experienced editor offered her services. All these were given free of charge. This degree of support continued with each new stage of the book, all the way through to the final printing.

In each case it was my strong desire and intention, combined with my willingness to receive, that focused universal energy to help create the desired outcome.

We all can use the power of creative intention to draw to ourselves whatever we require next for our healing and to attract whatever we desire in our life. Creative intention can also be used to find answers to questions. This technique is so powerful and works so well that we need to be very careful what we ask for. I always ask that what I receive be 'in my highest and best interest'.

Seven

THE HEALER

QUALITIES OF A GOOD HEALER

Qualities which enhance a healer's ability to create rapport and assist in the healing process include patience, trust and faith. These qualities apply both to how the healer feels about himself or herself and to how they relate to the person being assisted. Patience is the ability to slow down, when necessary, to match the pace most comfortable to the person receiving the healing. Trust allows the healer to continue the healing session even when energy shifts are not readily apparent. Faith in a power greater than the healer's personal energy invites support and assistance from the universal source. All of these skills develop over time. Please have patience with yourself, trust the learning process and have the faith that you are being divinely guided.

The ability to clearly observe details about someone's body — skin colour, skin temperature, posture and other indicators — is a valuable tool for gaining insight into their self-image, level of self-esteem and what they are currently experiencing. Another valuable asset is the skill and sensitivity to ask questions that will help a person to get in touch with their feelings. Skilled healers are proficient in the art of listening, not only to what is said, but also to what is unsaid.

Some healers are motivated by a desire to help fix or change other people. It is extremely important for healers to keep their own issues separate from the issues of those they work with. Most successful healers continue to focus on healing their own issues and make sure that they continue their healing process. When doing healing work, pray for clarity and ask that the healing be done for 'the highest good of all concerned'.

THE HEALER AS A CATALYST

Healing can be described as a shift or change in vibration. It occurs when an energy blockage is released or when the body takes in healing energy and moves to a higher vibrational level. The healer's main function is to act as a catalyst for healing. In acting as a catalyst the healer assists the person to open up to receiving healing energy and to accepting himself or herself and their own perfection.

Most of us have had the experience of the energy in our car battery being so weak that the car wouldn't start. To start the car, we have to call someone with a good battery and a set of jumper cables. When the jumper cables are attached to both batteries, the car with the low battery starts very easily.

Frequently, a person requesting healing is simply low on energy, which greatly reduces their own ability to move negative energy out of their body. They are like a car with a drained battery. Consider the healer as a fully charged battery and their two hands as a pair of jumper cables. The healer extends love, support and energy in much the same way as a charged car battery transmits energy to a drained battery. Once the vehicle is started, it no longer needs the extra energy provided by the fully charged battery and can be disconnected from it. This is also true of healing work. Once healing energy has been given to someone, they are no longer dependent upon the healer. The main objective is for the person receiving healing to be free, independent and self-reliant.

In reality, *all healing is self-healing*. The healer is present to encourage and assist the recipient to be open and allow the healing to occur. If the person is not open to receiving the healing, rarely will the healing occur. All of the techniques in this book are designed to build trust and to create a bridge between the healer and the person receiving the healing, so that the greatest possible benefits can result.

PRAYER TO BECOME A HEALER

Centre and ground yourself as best you can and when in a meditative state repeat the following prayer three times. It is more effective and more powerful if you are willing to say it three times, three times per day for thirty days. Allow yourself to feel the energy each time you say it.

Prayer

Mother/Father God, Holy Spirit, Archangel Michael and healing angels, I (your name) now call forth your energy and your power into this room. I (your name) now ask you to bless me and to bless my hands that I may become a pure channel for the healing energy. I pray that as this healing energy flows through me it blesses, cleanses and purifies both me and everyone I work with.

Please continue to guide and direct me each and every day of my life that I may be of service. I ask for all that occurs in my life to be in the highest and best interest of all concerned.

CENTRING/GROUNDING

It is very important for anyone working with healing energy to remain centred and grounded while the energy is flowing through them. People who are not grounded can feel very spacey at times or can even become disoriented. It is also very important to be working with the purest spiritual energy. The following visualisation is to be done prior to working with healing energy. It ensures that the healer will remain centred and grounded and allows the greatest opportunity for healing to occur.

In addition to centring and grounding you, this visualisation is effective for clearing your own energy field.

Visualisation

Visualise a large ball of energy, a shaft of intense golden or white light, coming down from God or the Universal Source. Visualise the top of your head opening to receive this energy and allow the energy to flow down through the top of your head. As this energy moves slowly down through your body, see and feel it blessing, cleansing and purifying your entire being on mental, physical, emotional and spiritual levels. Allow this pure energy to break up and wash away all blockages, negative patterns, doubts, fears and resistances you may have. Feel it pass down through the top of your head, continue down through your neck and into your heart. Now feel the energy continue to move from your heart downward to the base of your spine. Allow the energy to continue to move down and out your feet and flow deep into the earth.

Continue to move this ball of energy all the way to the centre of the earth and then visually connect it with the core of the earth. This helps ensure that you stay grounded. While remaining connected, bring the ball of energy back up through the bottoms of your feet and up into your heart. Feel the energy filling and purifying your heart. When your heart and entire body are full of this unconditional love and healing energy, send out a beam of healing energy from your heart and your hands to the person you are working with.

Allow yourself to relax, knowing that you are the vessel for the healing energy. Know that all you have to do is remain centred and allow the healing energy to flow through you. The energy knows what needs to be done and the best way to do it. In reality, there is very little that you need to do besides staying present. The healing energy goes where it is most needed. This centring process is as much about surrendering your ego and desires as anything else.

PROTECTION

It is very important — especially when first learning to work with energy — for you to protect and insulate yourself from the negative energy with which you might come in contact. Visualising hollow tubes in your body in which the energy is contained is one method. Another is to visualise yourself encased in a bubble of intense white light. This bubble is sealed and repels all negative energy. Another way is to visualise rings or bracelets around your wrists which act as an energy filter to block any negative energy from travelling up your arms and entering your body. Washing your hands with soap and water after working with each person is an excellent way of reminding yourself to release any negative energy you may have picked up.

In reality, if you do not feel the need to take on the pain and illnesses of others, you will not absorb any of their negative energy. The clearer you are that the people you are working with are not victims, the easier it will be for you to avoid taking on their pain. Remember that they have their own power, their own ability to heal themselves and that they need to take full responsibility for their lives. You, as a healer, are only assisting them in reclaiming their power and their health.

If you know within your own mind and heart that each and every person who comes to you has the ability to heal themself instantly, you will, by your support and confidence in them and their abilities, give them additional strength and courage to activate their own healing powers.

TAKING ON OTHER PEOPLE'S PAIN

Some healers who rely on other people for their self-worth or those who are very compassionate, sensitive and caring might believe they have to take on other people's aches and pains in order to help them heal. Such healers can spend a good portion of their time being sick, feeling drained or recovering from other people's ailments. This limits both the number of people they can assist and the clarity they can provide. You do not need to take on another person's issues in order to help. In fact, if you do not remain neutral, acting only as a catalyst, not only are you failing to honour and serve an individual, you are actually prolonging their condition.

As stated earlier, pain and illness are caused by energy blockages in the body, which indicate that something is out of balance. Blockages are unresolved issues. If you, as a healer, take on another's pain, you deprive them of the opportunity to learn valuable lessons and deny them the potential benefits of confronting and dealing with their issues. Pain is a message. The body is crying out that it can no longer compensate for the imbalance and desperately needs help. As a person faces and heals their issues, the imbalances naturally clear and the accompanying pain is automatically released.

In the past I wanted to take away the hurt and pain of everyone who came to me. Thinking I was helping people, I absorbed their pain and illnesses. As a result I became ill, I suffered and the people I worked with either did not heal, became ill again or re-created something worse in their lives. I learned the hard way that the best means of helping a person is to stay present, to listen, to provide support and to allow the healing energy to come through me without feeling responsible for the results achieved. I had to learn that the degree of healing a person receives is entirely their responsibility, not mine. Yes, it is important to be sensitive and to care about other people. However, when you start taking other people's pain, illness and lessons into your own body, you have gone beyond helping them and are serving neither them nor yourself.

NOTE: Children, especially those under the age of seven, and pets have wide-open energy fields and have no energetic boundaries. Being so open, they act as emotional sponges, absorbing pain, illness and negativity from those around them.

At times you might notice homes where the parents appear to be loving and happy, yet the pets and/or children keep getting sick or even die. In these cases always check to see if the pets or children are becoming ill from absorbing the unexpressed anger or negativity in the home. It is a well known fact that pets and children will process and act out these unexpressed emotions or become ill from absorbing them. Few, however, realise their sensitivity level or the amount of negativity they take into their body.

The cat described earlier in this book under 'Cancerous Tumour' might be a perfect example of this. Although the tumour I described melted away, the cat later died from other tumours. Was the cat absorbing the negativity from the family? I believe it was. The fact that the tumour I had worked on melted away confirms the power of healing energy. I am convinced that since the one tumour dissolved so quickly, the necessary amount of energy for a total healing was present. The cat, for some reason unknown to me, appears to have chosen not to heal completely. Healing is as much a choice as it is a process!

JUDGEMENT AND CRITICISM

For many years I lived in a black and white world: this was good, that was bad; this was right, that was wrong. I did my best to label everything I felt and experienced. After labelling and defining things, I put them into rigid boxes in my mind. There were no grey areas for me in those days. I was opinionated, rigid and negative. Using my know-it-all attitudes, I recklessly judged and criticised almost everyone, especially myself. In reality, I was scared and insecure.

Native Americans say that you cannot understand another person until you have walked a mile in their moccasins.

The wisdom in this saying is profound. Each one of us is a product of our genetic code, our experiences and our environment. This includes the physical home we were raised in, our social setting, our culture and the other people we grew up around. At times, it is easy to understand and accept others. At other times, people seem totally illogical.

As I have grown older — and wiser — I have learned that nothing is black or white, good or bad. It just is. The following parable illustrates my point.

The Old Farmer

An old man and his son were very poor and worked a small farm with only one horse to pull the plough. One day the horse ran away.

"How terrible," sympathised the neighbours. "What bad luck."

"Who knows whether it is bad luck or good luck," the farmer replied.

A week later, the horse returned from the mountains leading five wild mares into the barn.

"What wonderful luck!" said the neighbours.

"Good luck? Bad luck? Who knows?" answered the old man.

The next day the son, trying to tame one of the wild horses, fell and broke his leg.

"How terrible. What bad luck!"

"Bad luck? Good luck?"

Soon after this the army came to all the farms to take the young men to war. The farmer's son was of no use to them, so he was spared.

"Good? Bad?"

I am learning to live in the grey area, trusting that each of us is where we need to be for our own growth and healing and that each of us is doing the very best we can in any given moment. We are all being guided and led by a Spiritual Power whether we call it God, a Higher Power, Jesus, Holy Spirit or Universal Power. I am not always sure where I am going or what I am to be doing. However, what I do know is that I am doing the best I can in every moment. I listen and pay attention to what is presenting itself in my life and take full responsibility for how I respond to it. I am committed to healing myself more every day. As I do this, I realise that any criticism or judgement I make of myself and others only serves to separate me from the unconditional, all-encompassing love I feel growing inside me.

SEEING THE PERFECTION

Whenever we see an imperfection (note the judgement that something isn't perfect) and label it as such, we enhance it and give it power. With our judgement we create an energy picture, a mental image, thereby reinforcing the imperfection in our own mind. This is true even when we speak of an illness. It only adds to the problem by reinforcing the existence of the negative attributes (energy).

For example, every time someone says "I have cancer," they are stating an affirmation that labels and reinforces the existence of the illness. This is especially true if the person making the statement also has feelings of futility, depression and impending death associated with this disease. Strong emotions add energy, positive or negative, to everything a person says, thinks and does. All of these negative qualities are brought up and unconsciously amplified every time the person discusses their illness. If you, as a listener, have any negative thoughts in your own mind regarding the illness or imperfections of others, it only adds to the problem, slowing and complicating the healing process.

A person can shift the energy and the focus into a positive direction by positive reinforcing statements: "Last week I was diagnosed with cancer. I really know that if I created it, I can heal it. I am totally committed to my own healing." If the emotions and the mind are kept positive, there is a good chance that the cancer's progress will be arrested and reverse itself.

One key to healing is to see the person as perfect and whole. Whenever you see another person as less than whole, or less than the perfection they truly are, you are standing in the way of their real healing. Healing occurs more quickly and easily when you can see the God or good within each person. The more you honour the people you work with, even in the quiet of your own heart and mind, the easier and faster they will heal. If you see the person in his or her absolute magnificence and total perfection, you actually help their self-empowerment and speed up the healing process tremendously. Just visualising and holding the image of perfection is one of the greatest gifts you can ever give another person. This was demonstrated very dramatically in the healing of Eagle Feather.

UNCONDITIONAL LOVE

Unconditional love is loving someone absolutely and totally without any reservation. Unconditional love is neither critical nor judgemental, and has no expectations, attachments or fixed pictures as to how things should be. It is a state of pure love. Watching the adoration of a mother with a newborn baby is an example of the energy of unconditional love. The baby is not expected to act or to be a certain way. The baby is loved just because it exists, especially during its first few days.

As children few of us were raised in an environment of unconditional love. Even as adults, whether married or not, most people only rarely experience this deep level of love. Society, our culture and the work environment impose so many rules, regulations and expectations as to how we should act and the way things should be said and done, that it is very difficult to feel accepted — much less loved. Only once in a great while does a person experience unconditional love in the world, yet in all the great teachings there are many stories about miracles created by the power of this kind of love.

The great masters and spiritual teachers knew that a caring look, a warm smile, a gentle touch, a kind word could create a healing. As a person heals and lets their heart open, and allows the love, acceptance and support within to reach out and connect with another person, they create miracles. This is true even if the person receiving this love does not consciously feel it or is unaware of their own capacity to love. Unconditional love and acknowledgement can totally heal and transform a person.

Unconditional love can heal faster and more completely than any drug or surgery. Jesus, Mother Teresa, Gandhi and many other masters knew this truth and with their love literally transformed those they met.

ACCEPTANCE

It is very important that healers be able to accept everything that is told to them. Many people have been abused mentally, emotionally, physically and spiritually. To assist them in their healing process, you must be able to work with them without judging them because, in reality, there is nothing to judge. Any judgements you have or make will only get in the way and deter the healing process. If you feel judgemental or critical, the individual coming to you for the healing will be able to sense your judgement. Anything less than unconditional love will sabotage the effectiveness of a healing session.

It is important to be gentle and understanding with everyone who comes to you for healing. When you come from a place of unconditional love — loving regardless of race, colour, creed, gender, background, action or inaction

— a place of complete acceptance, then you create a space for healing. Acceptance and unconditional love create a sacred space.

Be clear also that acceptance, like forgiveness, does not involve full agreement with, nor does it condone, all acts and behaviours. Rather, it is a lack of judgement of other human beings who are dealing with their life challenges, their learning paths and their own healing process in the best way that they know.

NON-ATTACHMENT TO RESULTS

In the western world, people learn to compete at an early age and they suffer the consequences of that programming throughout their lives. Most of us are programmed to obtain results and are motivated to achieve success. These programmed attitudes and skills work against a healer. To be a healer requires the development and use of other skills. Setting an intention or desire for healing is normal and appropriate. However, when either the healer or the person receiving the healing becomes attached to a specific result and strives for that particular outcome, the energy becomes disruptive.

If you, as a healer, need to prove yourself on any level you are only detracting from the purity of the healing. By imposing your needs for approval and results onto others, you introduce a disruptive energy pattern that is similar to the energy of expectation, violation and abuse that many people experienced in childhood. If you are not clear with the healing energy, you may be perpetuating the same type of violation that was the root cause of the dis-ease in the first place.

When the healer remains unattached to a specific outcome, the person receiving the healing is allowed the freedom to change for themself rather than changing to please the healer. If the person changes to please someone else, the healing will usually be only superficial and any positive results will probably be short-lived. Developing the skill of non-attachment will greatly assist those you work with as well as helping you realise your full potential in healing work. Any energy other than unconditional love and acceptance can feel like violation to the person, even when it is meant to help. This is especially true if they were violated as a child.

Please remember that healing takes place best when you let healing energy come through you and remain unattached to the outcome. This allows the energy to flow naturally and permits the person to heal at their own pace.

INTUITION — THE GOLDEN GIFT

Intuition is one of a healer's greatest assets. The ability to listen to and hear your inner guidance, to sense or see images in your mind or to be guided by an inner knowing is a very special gift. At times you may be guided to say or do things that seem strange to the logical mind. When used appropriately, this guidance gives you the opportunity to leap beyond the normal senses and gain insights in a way that could very easily lead to a breakthrough in a person's healing process. Intuition goes far beyond book knowledge; it comes from your own deep inner knowing, not from your thinking.

Inner guidance may come in the form of a feeling, a picture or a voice. Meditation, or any practice that helps to quiet down the mental chatter and clear stray thoughts from the mind, will assist you in hearing and feeling this intuitive guidance when it comes. Asking and praying for inner guidance to become an active part of your life and to assist in your healing and the healing of others can greatly accelerate the process of opening up. Regardless of your current skill level, trust that your ability is indeed developing and allow time for this gift to grow. The more you use it, the faster it will develop.

My intuition — my inner guidance — is accessed when I mentally and emotionally disengage, take a few deep breaths, relax, quiet my mind and go inside to ask "What is really going on here? How can I help this person? What am I to do or say?" Many times when I am very relaxed and actively listening to a person, an image or impression will come to me; other times I will hear words. Some people I know smell fragrances or see colours. In most cases, the guidance received will be the key to unlocking the challenge.

Often when assisting someone I will get the impression of a parent or an earlier age in the person's life. When asked, "What happened between you and your (father/mother)?" "What do you want to say to your (father/mother)?" or "What happened when you were (age)?", the person will frequently burst into tears. The remembering of a past event and the completion of it releases the blocked energy, thereby facilitating the healing process.

In 1986 I met a man in Skagway, Alaska who was experiencing a recurring pain in his foot. He explained that he could not remember injuring his foot, however he was aware that it had not bothered him prior to his moving near the ocean.

As I listened I relaxed and in my mind clearly saw the inside of the bow of a small wooden boat with a coil of rope on the floor. As I watched I asked myself what this meant and although I did not get a picture immediately, I sensed that this person, in what appeared to be a past lifetime, was a fisherman who had been standing near the bow. Somehow his foot had become entangled in the rope and he was either hurt or dragged overboard and drowned. After sharing my insight and doing an aura cleansing the pain went away and to the best of my knowledge never returned. The amazing part for me was that this discussion and the insight happened while I was driving on a winding narrow road.

When learning to access your intuition make sure you ask the person you are working with for permission to share what you are receiving. After communicating your insight always ask if what you have shared has any meaning for them. In all cases, make sure to approach this by asking questions rather than making statements. This will allow the person to go inside and check their own feelings. Most people will register a 'true' response by some type of physical or emotional reaction in their body — a tightness in the pit of the stomach, a muscle jerk or goosebumps on the skin. Regardless of the reaction from the person you are working with, remember how and what you are intuitively receiving, so that over time you can observe the accuracy of your impressions. You may even wish to keep a journal of these intuitive insights.

The best healers are guided from within. It takes a willingness to practise and accept honest feedback in order to learn to listen to and trust the information you are receiving intuitively.

SPIRITUAL GUIDES AND HELPERS

I find it extremely empowering to begin a session with a prayer, calling in God, Holy Spirit, my spiritual guides, teachers and the spiritual healers who work with me to assist in the healing session. I also ask for the presence of the guides of the person receiving the healing.

Depending upon your belief systems and your willingness to accept help, you may wish to call forth the energy of God, Holy Spirit, Jesus, Mother Mary, Mother Earth, Sophia, Archangel Michael, the Great Spirit, your Higher Power, the Universal Energy or one or more of the Saints. It is important to call in both masculine and feminine energies so a balance is achieved. People who are sensitive to energy can actually feel each energy come in as its help is requested.

I always ask that the guides, teachers and helpers who come to assist me in the healings be on the master level of the white light or higher, and be aligned with God's will, God's love, God's truth and God's wisdom.

After the healing is over, thank the spiritual guides and healers for their assistance. Then ask God to bless the spiritual guides and healers for assisting and release them so that they can go where they are most needed.

In my experience, despite all my doubts, fears and insecurities, the spiritual helpers have always come when called upon.

Eight

DIALOGUING: THE INTERACTION BETWEEN HEALER AND RECIPIENT

ASKING PERMISSION

Many healers, in their exuberance to help, rush into working with the energy in ways that some people, especially those who have experienced abuse and boundary violations, may find offensive. Unfortunately, the energy of exuberance may be similar in intensity to the energy with which some people were originally abused. This similarity can trigger and throw a person into even deeper trauma and pain. On occasions, this type of triggering may become a tool which, when handled properly, can be used to uncover and release the trauma that has accumulated in a person. In many cases, however, the person becomes very angry with the healer and sees the healer as being similar to their abuser. If the person feels this way, they may be reluctant ever to work with that healer again.

It took me many years, and numerous errors, before I learned to slow down and check things out with the person I am working with. I have learned to ask if a person feels comfortable with my putting my hands on them, even on a seemingly safe place such as their back. My goal is to have the person willingly and actively work with me in assisting their healing process. Asking permission helps to create a safe, open and trusting relationship between the healer and the person being worked with.

Remember, it is always better to go a little slower than to move too fast and risk traumatising a person, causing them to shut down even more. Pushing someone too far beyond their comfort zone without their permission or taking away their problems by your personal power will usually result in their relapsing into the same or a similar situation or developing something even worse to deal with.

ACTIVE PARTICIPATION

Some people want to receive a healing in the same way they would have a massage — that is, receiving passively and expecting the healer to do most, if not all, of the work.

This passive approach does not allow for the maximum empowerment and support of the person receiving the healing. If you do not actively include people in every aspect of their own healing process, you are denying them a very valuable opportunity to take charge of their health and demonstrate their own ability to heal themselves. Once empowered with this knowledge a person can heal many more areas of their life than just the current issue.

Active participation includes asking a person what they are feeling, what they are seeing, where the pain is, how they would describe it and for any other details they can tell you. Always encourage them to participate actively and assume as much responsibility as possible during their session, even encouraging them to direct the energy. Ask them to visualise with you the negative energy being pulled out and the positive energy flowing in. By frequently asking the person what they are feeling, seeing and sensing, you keep them actively participating in what is going on. When you do this, they tend to stay present and current with what is happening. The greater the active responsibility a person takes in their own healing process, the easier that process will be.

The more the person can feel their pain, describe the energy blockages and visualise the energy flowing, the easier it is to locate the blockages in the body and identify the challenge. Once the challenge is identified, it is fairly easy to release and heal the blockages. When working with someone who is communicating with you closely, you will know instantly if the desired changes are occurring and if the way you are working with the energy is actually shifting the blockages. In these cases the person can tell you when the energy blockage has partially or fully released because they can usually see, feel or sense it in their body. With this feedback, you may even find ways to improve your own healing techniques. The more a person receiving a healing can see the pictures in vivid colours, hear the sounds, smell the odours, taste the tastes and feel the sensations — in other words, the more they remain totally present within their own physical body and actively participate in the experience — the easier will it be for the healing to occur.

One of the benefits of this active participation is that the person is facing their illnesses or challenges head on. In doing this, they are confronting their fears and are allowing the healer to support them, while both are working *together* to focus and direct the healing energy.

Including a person in their own healing process — by asking questions and having them describe what they are seeing and feeling — is one of the most powerful tools that a healer can employ. It will greatly enhance the results of the healing.

ASKING QUESTIONS

Many people are accustomed to making statements as opposed to asking questions. While doing healing work I have found that by asking questions I do not trigger a person's ego and personality defences nearly as much as when I make statements. Asking questions gets the person being healed involved, which is very important in creating trust and open communication.

At the beginning of a healing session, spend time with

the person and ask questions such as: "What would you like to work on?" "What results would you like to achieve?" "If your life did change, how would you use your life or live it differently?" These questions cause the person to focus on an outcome. This activates creative intention, aligning the mind to support the overall healing work to be done.

While doing the healing, frequently ask the person you are working with what they are feeling within their body, where they are feeling it, what colours they are seeing and what emotions are coming up for them. This feedback provides information as to how the person is responding to the energy and also gives insights into the possible next steps in their healing process.

Our prehistoric ancestors who lived off the land as hunter-gatherers relied heavily on their feelings and instincts. Their very survival depended upon their being in touch with their feelings and the sensations in their bodies. In today's highly structured, mechanised society we have lost touch with ourselves and have suppressed many of our feelings. We have numbed our senses with drugs, alcohol, cigarettes and television. Asking questions about what a person is experiencing helps them get back in touch with their feelings and prompts them to notice sensations in their physical body.

Although at first the person receiving healing may have to stop and search for their feelings, they can be found. Feelings are the key to the healing process. They help to identify what is going on in the body and how the energy is changing. By asking questions you direct and encourage the person to stay in touch with their feelings and remain conscious of what is going on in their body. Encouraging communication of any changes in the way they feel during the healing session helps them to claim the changes and provides both the conscious and subconscious minds with hard data to confirm that a change has occurred. This validates the healing process. Frequently, a person will see, feel and experience most of the energy shifts that I sense before I mention them.

If I receive an image or impression of the issue a person is working on, I might ask questions like: "I have a feeling about the area we are working on. May I share it with you? My sense of the situation is ________. Is it possible that you are feeling some anger over the situation?" Asking and checking things out — as opposed to telling — invites people to go within to review things for themselves, to ask themselves questions, to be honest with themselves and hopefully to gain insights into the situation. As they do this, they might gain more clarity or see more of the picture than you do.

Remember, if the person you are working with does not agree with your guidance, that is okay. Trust yourself and follow your guidance on what to do. If you do not have the person's permission, be sure you do this without pushing or challenging them. Before giving feedback, ask the person you are working with if they want to know what you are sensing and then — only when you get permission — share what you are picking up. This sharing could increase a person's deeper awareness of what they are going through. Be aware that at times someone may not be in touch with what is going on in their life; at other times they may be in denial of the situation. In many cases, days or weeks later, the person may call and confirm the accuracy of your intuitive knowing.

FEELINGS

There is a saying in the healing profession that 'you can't heal what you can't feel'. Unfortunately, most of us growing up in today's society — especially men — have been taught to control, suppress and hide our emotions, feelings or sensitivities. Societal pressure has pushed us into shutting down to avoid feeling emotional pain. The media and the marketing and advertising industries have seduced us into numbing ourselves with food, drugs, cigarettes, alcohol, sex, television, overwork and countless other diversions.

It is only when we give ourselves permission to start feeling again, that we are able to begin the healing process. As we heal and learn to set appropriate limits and boundaries for ourselves and others, we are able to live as sensitive human beings without giving up who we really are or allowing other people to hurt or control us.

When a person's feelings have been suppressed for a long time and they begin to express them again, at first they will tend to do so in an unskilled manner. This is to be expected, since they have not used this ability for some time. Within a short time, however, and with practice, they will begin to express their feelings comfortably and at a reasonably skilled level most of the time.

It is okay for each individual to feel all of their feelings and to be the sensitive person he or she truly is. In fact, it is mandatory in order to remain healthy.

ENCOURAGING A PERSON TO TRUST, FEEL AND TALK

Three of the most prominent behavioural rules of dysfunctional families are: don't trust, don't feel and don't talk. It is totally logical, then, that the goal of the healer is to help people trust themselves, identify and feel all of their feelings and feel safe enough to communicate and to share from the heart. If a person feels safe talking about what they have experienced and is able, without fear of judgement or criticism, to openly share their pain, their shame and their concerns, healing will occur much more easily and quickly.

While working with a person, encourage them to feel. This can be achieved by asking them to move their attention into any areas of pain and discomfort in the body. I do this by asking people to breathe into and fully feel the pain; I also ask if they are getting any pictures, words or feelings associated with the pain. In my experience, if someone is willing to breathe into and touch the depth of their pain for even one second, the energy of the trauma and the blockage will be released. Pain and emotional blockages, once they are faced, confronted and dealt with, usually heal quickly. Once healed, these issues might seem trivial when compared to the problems and resistance they created in a person's life.

I have experienced many people who were petrified and in terror of facing an issue or memory. In most cases, once they have confronted the issue they are able to move quickly through it, usually within minutes. One woman, Phyllis, although she knew she needed help and wanted me to work with her, avoided scheduling a session for a year. When she finally did come to see me, she was almost hysterical with fear. Once she allowed me to start working with her, the breakthrough took only minutes. Using visualisation, I had her close her eyes, surrender into the fear and recall the memory of the event that created it. As the picture of the experience became more clear, I assisted her in seeing the decisions she had made as a result of this experience. I then asked her if those decisions now served her or hindered her. Next, we looked at what decisions were more appropriate for her to make. Finally she chose to keep only the best decisions. She could not believe that the issue that had controlled her life for almost thirty years ook only minutes to heal.

When a person has feelings and emotions coming up, encourage and support them in moving into the fears rather than away from them, thereby avoiding or suppressing them. Statements such as: "It's okay," "Allow the feelings to come up," "Breathe into the pain," "Surrender into the feelings," "It's okay, I'm here," "You're safe," "Stay with your feelings," "Allow yourself to go all the way through this," support a person through their fears and into their pain. The confidence and skill to work with someone in this way increases with time. Working with other healers is an excellent way to share information and gain valuable experience.

Although it is important for a person to talk about what they are experiencing, you must be careful that they do not stay in their head and get lost in the drama of their story. Questions can be used to help get a person out of their head and back in touch with their feelings. Some of these questions are: "What are you feeling now?" "How do you feel about what happened to you?" "What are you feeling in your body?" "What sensations are you feeling in your body?" "Where are you feeling that in your body?" The more a person can be brought back into their feelings and encouraged to feel their emotions, as well as the pain, the easier it will be for them to free these blocked emotions.

SURRENDERING — LETTING GO

Healing is a process of letting go, surrendering, fully feeling and releasing all pain, fears and blockages. Only after fully feeling their emotions can someone release the energy locked up in the experience.

Unresolved past experiences greatly influence what a person feels now. Healing occurs when they are honest with themself, face the fact that they have been hurt and willingly feel their pain and anger. Remember, the real key to the healing process and to change is when a person allows themself to feel all their feelings, to let go, to surrender and to relax into their pain — to cry and to feel all of their feelings without judgement.

I tell people that if they are willing to fully feel the depth of their pain for even one second it will free the trapped energy, much like the quick release of air when a pin is stuck into a blown up balloon.

Nine

Advanced Skills and Tools for Healing: Understanding and Supporting the Healing Process

THE POWER OF OUR WORDS

Words send out a powerful message — much more powerful than is usually understood. We continually send these messages out to those around us, as well as to our own conscious and subconscious minds. Words can be used either to strengthen and empower or to undermine the self or others (see 'Creative Intention', 'Negative Self-Talk' and 'Anchoring'). When we use positive statements, we reinforce our self-image and self-esteem. Positive statements encourage us and help us to build a healthy relationship with ourselves and the world around us. They confirm our value as humans. Few people realise that words can actually poison and pollute the thinking, the energy fields and the body, in much the same way that toxic chemicals can damage the physical body.

Our mind is much like a computer. There is a saying in the computer field: "Garbage in — garbage out." I will make an additional statement: "Wonderful things in — wonderful things out." The mind can be programmed, like a computer, and is only as good as the information entered into it. If we enter erroneous or limited information, we will reach faulty conclusions. If we enter good, clear information, our conclusions will be accurate and we will have a more realistic picture of how the world operates. The more positive and loving the input that we give our mind, the more peaceful, prosperous and successful our life will be.

Here are some examples of positive and negative words and statements:

Positive approach	Negative approach
challenge	problem
eager	anxious
exhilarated	scared
bless	damn
prosperous	broke
when	if
I am doing it now	I'll try
I can/I will do it	I can't
I will remember	I forgot
I apologise	I am sorry
misplaced	lost
concerned	worried

'But' is a frequently used word that discounts every positive word that is said before it. For example, I have heard people say, "I am doing better, *but* I know it won't last long." The words "I am doing better" are discounted by the word 'but' and the real message becomes "I know it won't last long."

When listening to someone who frequently uses the word 'but' I sometimes get the feeling of riding in a car with a driver who alternates between stepping on the gas and the brakes. Listen to how people use the word 'but' and notice whether they are giving away their power, stopping themselves or discounting the positive messages they started to give themselves.

THE MIND — NEGATIVE WORDS

The conscious mind has the ability to distinguish between a positive word and a negative one. This means that when someone is told not to do something, the conscious mind understands and can follow the instructions.

The subconscious mind, however, does not process or integrate negative words — such as 'no', 'not', 'never' — into the word pictures it creates. This means that whenever people give themselves or someone else a command using a negative word, it goes directly into the subconscious as though it were positive.

Telling someone "Don't think about a pink elephant" causes the conscious mind first to create the image of the pink elephant. It has to do this to establish a reference point, so that it understands what is being talked about. Once the picture is created, it tries to erase it, in order to fulfil the request. Obviously, if you want to help someone eliminate a negative pattern, you do not want to emphasise the pattern more strongly in the person's mind by creating a vivid picture that will not serve them.

An affirmation such as "I'm not going to get fatter" translates in the subconscious mind as, "I'm going to get fatter." A better way to reprogram the mind would be to say, "Every day in every way I am becoming slimmer and slimmer." Another example, "I'm not going to have cancer any more," translates to "I'm going to have cancer." A better phrase to use would be, "Every day in every way I am getting healthier and healthier." These statements will reprogram both the conscious and the subconscious mind in a positive way.

In a recent television scene a man in a coma was being told by several people, including his adolescent son, "Don't die, don't die, please, don't die on me." They had no idea that they were actually programming this unconscious man to die. A much better encouragement would have been, "You're doing fine, you're going to make it. Your body is healing very quickly; you will regain consciousness very soon now."

The mind operates in a consistent, systematic way, very much like a computer. The more a healer understands and works with its natural, functioning process, the easier it will be to assist others to release old negative habits and patterns and replace them with healthy positive ones.

NEGATIVE SELF-TALK

Negative self-talk, the chatter in the mind, is one of the most destructive habits we have, because it is almost impossible to shut it off or walk away from it. This chatter is with us every day and night, heckling us and tearing down our self-image and self-esteem. Chatter can originate from a variety of sources: parents, siblings, authority figures, the self and others.

Frequently parents or others impose expectations upon us or use us as an escape valve to vent their anger, hurt or frustration in life. This abuse may be expressed verbally or non-verbally. Over time comments like "You're ugly," "You're fat," "You're stupid," "You can't do that," "It won't work anyway, why bother," "You don't matter," "Nothing you do will ever matter," "No one really cares about you," "You're not important," "You're not good enough," "You'll never succeed" can seriously weaken and even destroy our self-image and self-esteem. This is especially true in the case of children and others who are not emotionally strong enough to defend themselves. Children have psychically open energy fields and they accept what 'big people' say about them as absolute truth. Eventually they internalise these abusive statements and start repeating them to themselves.

The effect of negative self-talk becomes even more destructive when we accept those abusive statements of "*You* are ______" and internalise them as "*I* am ______." In this process, the judgements and criticism of others are accepted into our self-talk. A critical point is reached when, rather than repeating others' words in our mind in the second person — 'you are' — we begin to repeat them from a first-person — 'I am' — point of view. Someone tells us, "You're stupid," and our mind changes this to "I'm stupid." This shift is not subtle. It is a major shift during which we internalise — accept into our conscious and subconscious — the falsehood about who we are.

Reversing and eliminating negative self-talk takes commitment, determination, practice and the willingness to accept that abusers and other people are wrong. The more we can confront our negative self-talk — telling it to 'stop', telling the people behind the voices that they are wrong — and start positively reclaiming our wounded self, the faster we will heal.

Affirmations, journal-keeping, meditating and inner child work support the journey back to total health. We can quiet or eliminate our negative self-talk and stand up to the voices in our head by yelling out loud or silently in our mind "Stop," "Be quiet," "Your work is finished," "It's time for you to go now!" This willingness to confront self-talk is critical to subduing negative programs. A friend shared that when he heard a negative voice in his head, he simply, very calmly, told it, "Thank you for sharing — now be quiet and go away."

There are other approaches to healing negative self-talk. You can meditate and ask for God or Higher Power to help quiet your mind. Another approach is to combine journal-keeping and meditating to get in touch with and communicate with the source of the negative self-talk, asking where it came from and what it wants. When you know these answers, you can heal this voice by praying for its healing and release, and start programming the message you really want to have.

Conscious breathing, breathing slowly and deeply, can also change the energy. On the in-breath, say to yourself,

"I am"; as you exhale say, "Peace". Repeat this for at least 5-15 minutes. This provides positive programming and self-talk which changes the focus of your mind and can lessen the power of negative self-talk.

Another approach is to pay close attention to your self-talk. If it becomes negative, change your focus and engage in an activity that demands your full attention and physical strength, such as jogging, swimming, playing tennis or sailing. You can also change your focus by helping someone else in need.

In my own life, and especially while writing this book, I have struggled with my own negative self-talk such as, "You're not good enough," "You'll never be good enough," "What you say and do doesn't really matter," "No one really cares," "It will never be good enough," "Everything you say has already been said by someone else." Writing this book, and making a commitment to complete it, brought up a tremendous number of negative childhood memories with all of the negative self-talk and accompanying physical and emotional traumas. I did my best to stay focused on the project, while working with friends, colleagues, other healers and numerous other support people to walk through my resistance. I am happy to report that this project also brought much joy to my life and will continue to do so for years to come.

ANCHORING

Anchoring is a term that means creating a stimulus-response connection. Once this connection is created, a person is automatically activated, without any conscious awareness, every time the stimulus occurs. Pavlov, a famous scientist, created a stimulus-response reaction in dogs by ringing a bell every time he fed them. Eventually he rang the bell without feeding them. When the bell rang, the dogs salivated just as if they were being fed. The stimulus-response connection between the bell and the feeding had been made at such a deep level that the response was unconscious, immediate and uncontrollable. Another example of anchoring is the story of the baby elephant and the chain.

Humans respond to stimulus in the same way. An example of negative anchoring is when children are given unconditional love only when they are sick or hurt; as adults they will automatically become sick or hurt whenever they want or need unconditional love. They may continue to repeat this unconscious action throughout their entire lives, never consciously understanding why they get sick.

Another example of negative anchoring is when parents give a child food whenever he or she is scared, hurt or troubled and tell them that this will make them feel better. After three or four times, such a pattern becomes ingrained and can have devastating effects on a person's weight for the rest of their life. They are taught to stuff down their feelings while stuffing in food. A person programmed in this way has not been taught to feel their feelings, to express them or to work through them in a healthy way.

Positive anchoring occurs when a reward is given upon successful completion of a task, such as when animal trainers reward their seals, dolphins or dogs with food for successfully performing a trick. Everyone can use this same approach to positive programming by rewarding themselves with special treats for the successful completion of a task. These special rewards could be a verbal congratulation to oneself, a pat on the back, going to a movie, to the beach, out to dinner or even on vacation. Such rewards encourage the completion of the task.

ANCHORING — EMBEDDED COMMANDS

Embedded commands are statements and phrases which go directly into the subconscious mind. Usually these are made by an authority figure with intensity and without warning. When delivered in this way such statements can easily slip directly into the subconscious, bypassing the filters of the conscious mind with little or no resistance. Embedded commands are especially destructive if the receiver is not expecting a forceful negative comment and is caught off guard. Unfortunately, once these comments are in the subconscious, they are automatically accepted as facts. The negative message is especially intensified if these statements are made by an authority figure such as a parent, teacher, boss, doctor or therapist.

Negative embedded commands or interjections — such as, "You need help," "You're sicker than you think," "You're going to die," "You'll never amount to anything," "You're stupid," "You're dumb," etc. — can devastate our self-image and self-esteem, especially when they are communicated with strong negative emotion. The first part of us to be affected will be our mind. Then our emotions and physical body will suffer from the effects of the negativity. It is at this point that our confidence is destroyed and eventually our spirit is broken.

Positive embedded commands can have an uplifting effect and can speed the healing process. Statements such as, "You're in better shape than you realise," "You are almost through this one," etc. can positively reinforce a healing session. Other positive embedded commands — such as an instructor's yelling "Go!" to someone about to do a firewalk or rope climbing — may appear to help a person; in reality they take away the person's sense of their *own* timing.

AFFIRMATIONS

Affirmations are words or word pictures, written or spoken, declaring a specific outcome. This is different from visualisation, which is the creation of a vivid picture in the mind. Affirmations are a form of programming and can be used very effectively, especially after a healing has released negative energy and old belief patterns. Affirmations are more powerful when you say them frequently, at least once a day, over an extended period of time. They are most effective when you say them as you first wake in the morning, at lunchtime and as the last thing you do before going to sleep at night. The more times you say an affirmation, especially in the early morning and late at night, the more easily it will penetrate the subconscious. Saying an affirmation morning, noon and night, repeating it three times at each sitting and doing this for 30 days can produce life-changing results.

The mind and body may go into resistance as the affirmation starts to change your perception. This resistance might take the form of getting tired, feeling discouraged (like it won't help anyway) or getting distracted so you don't follow through. Continue to say the affirmation for the full 30 days. If you miss a day or a sitting, continue the affirmation without allowing yourself to become frustrated or disgusted. Just pick up where you left off. Remember, some resistance is normal and natural. It shows where your negative programming exists.

Examples of affirmations are:

"I am getting better and better every day, in every way."

"I am a whole and perfect child of God."

"I am perfect just the way I am and I choose to continue to grow and evolve into my full potential."

"Spirit goes before me making my way easy, harmonious and successful."

"I (*your name*) am now willing to love, honour and respect myself at least as much as I am willing to love, honour and respect others."

FORGIVENESS

Forgiveness is another important key in the healing process. Extending forgiveness does not imply or infer agreeing with, condoning or minimising any violation that has occurred; nor does it mean establishing a close relationship with the person involved or even seeing them again. Rather, it is looking beyond the actions and seeing the perfection of that person's Spirit or soul. The purpose of the earth experience is to actively live life, to learn from each experience and then to make appropriate choices. Forgiveness acknowledges the possibility of a person's making a mistake and, at some point in time, realising they have made a mistake, learning from it and changing. When we forgive someone, we hold the creative intention of that person's perfection — rather than accentuating the negative aspects of their imperfections.

When we remain in judgement, condemnation, fear, hurt, anger or resentment, we stay hooked into the individual who hurt us. In addition, this keeps the negative emotions and negative energy flowing until they are released.

Anger and resentment are poisons which create toxic effects in the body. When we hold on to anger and resentment we are hurting only ourself — not the person who hurt us. This negative, toxic energy over time manifests into disease. By forgiving, we release ourself from the cycle of anger and revenge and we release the toxic energy from our body.

NOTE: This is the reason some people go through a healing crisis after they have made a major breakthrough in their healing process. Self-care during a healing crisis includes drinking lots of liquids, resting and staying away from stressful situations. Please remember that a healing crisis is the sign of a major, positive healing and is *not* a cause for panic.

When a person can move more deeply into their emotions they will usually burst into tears because of the pain and disappointment that is being released. They may sometimes feel afraid that they will be violated again. In this case do your best to reinforce their confidence by reassuring them that they can take care of themself now: they are older and stronger, they can say no and can set appropriate limits and boundaries. Remind them they are not the same person now as when they were violated. (Review 'Stuck in Time' section)

Forgiveness breaks the energy connection and the anger cycle between the abuser and the abused. Forgiveness also helps to break the cycle of being the victim and assists the person in taking command over their own energy.

Everyone has said and done things that they regret. Many times, they wish they could take back these things. What if other people were not willing to forgive us and move on with the process of life? Everyone has at some time gone back to apologise for their actions, seeking forgiveness. What if no one ever forgave anyone — what would life be like, with everyone carrying all that anger and resentment? Would anyone ever have a best friend again?

There are stories of Jesus and other great teachers spending time with murderers, prostitutes and thieves. Were they not offering forgiveness to these people for their past deeds and asking them to forgive themselves, open their hearts and come home — 'back into society' — in a new way.

In forgiveness a person is seen as a pure, perfect, loving soul who has themself been hurt, violated and abused. Because of this history, which has been passed down the family line through generations, the person has developed dysfunctional behaviour. This is the only way they know of being in the world; it is the only role model they have had. In most cases, the abuse committed is identical to that which the abuser experienced as a child. If you focus on this negative aspect, you are only perpetuating and feeding the negative. By forgiving the soul — the spirit — you are making a wake-up call, sending unconditional love which might spark movement in a positive direction. In either case forgiveness releases the person who has been hurt and allows them to get on with their life without carrying the 'heavy excess baggage' of hurt, pain and negative emotions.

There was an assassination attempt on the Pope some years ago; the Pope was seriously injured. Upon his recovery from the shooting he went to the prison cell of his would-be assassin. Against the recommendation of his advisors, he asked to be left alone with the person. Was the Pope looking beyond the act and seeing the person's troubled soul? I believe he was forgiving the soul of this person.

Forgiveness affirmations, because they usually involve specific people, are more powerful when you use a person's name.

Forgiveness Affirmations:

1. I (*your name*) now forgive (*person's name*) for hurting me. I feel that what you did to me was wrong and hurt me deeply. I (*your name*) bless and release (*person's name*) to their highest good and I bless and release myself to my highest good right now! And so it is.

2. I (*your name*) absolutely and totally forgive myself for (*action*). I forgive myself right now!

3. I (*your name*) absolutely and totally forgive (*person's name*) for (*action or deed*). I forgive them right now!

4. I (*your name*) now forgive everyone who has ever hurt me on any level and in any way from the beginning of time. I absolutely and totally forgive them right now!

5. I (*your name*) now ask for forgiveness from everyone I have ever hurt on any level and in any way from the beginning of time. I ask for and accept this forgiveness right now. I (*your name*) now absolutely and totally forgive myself for whatever I have done.

6. I (*your name*) now forgive myself for all the pain and suffering I have caused myself on all levels in all ways since the beginning of time. I forgive myself right now!

7. I (*your name*) am now willing to release the need for (*name of addiction, pain, fear or problem*) in my life. I (*your name*) release it now, accepting and trusting God, Holy Spirit and the process of life to assist me to heal and to meet all my needs and desires in a healthy way.

VISUALISATION / GUIDED IMAGERY

Visualisation is either the creation of a new, vivid picture in the mind or the process of recalling a past experience through guided imagery. When used to create healing or to manifest a specific outcome, visualisation works best by creating vivid, three-dimensional colour images in the mind, employing as many of the senses as possible. This means full-colour moving pictures with sounds, smells, tastes and feelings. When these senses are activated, the subconscious mind can more easily accept the visualisation as an actual reality.

Once we learn the technique of visualisation, we can use this ability to create a vivid motion picture in the mind to help us remember and re-experience past events. With this approach we can gain insights into the challenges and pain in our own and others' lives. We can even use guided imagery to unlock those memories which have been blocked from the conscious mind. Both visualisation and guided imagery can be used as powerful tools to reprogram and repattern the mind by placing positive pictures in it. In fact, the mind cannot tell the difference between guided imagery, visualisation and reality.

Most people experience times of drifting off and needing to stop for a moment to remember who and where they are. During these times — when daydreaming, while watching a good movie or even while dreaming during sleep — people become so engrossed in what is going on that the mind cannot tell the illusion from the reality. This ability of the mind to create vivid motion pictures, to accept these pictures as reality, to erase the past and to reprogram negative experiences is the reason why the use of visualisation is so valuable.

Although the visualisation technique is most powerful when working directly with a skilled healer, you can also guide yourself through the process. Commercially available audio and video tapes can be used as aids in creating positive visualisations. (See list at back of book.)

COLOURS

Different colours have distinct vibrations that can be used to enhance the healing process. Favoured healing colours are emerald green, white, gold, violet and pink. Emerald green is the colour of healing and of the heart centre. White represents purity and spirituality. Gold represents wisdom and enlightenment. Violet represents transformation and transmutation. Pink represents unconditional love. In many of the paintings of saints and other holy figures, these colours are prominent.

Have the person you are working with visualise a healing colour flowing into or through their body. Have them experience this colour entering the area of pain or blockage, saturating the problem area, breaking up and then washing away all the pain and negative patterns. After the negativity has melted and been washed clear, have them visualise the healing colour that they relate to the most filling up the area that needs healing.

When visualising negative energy, I usually see the colours red, murky brown or black — the colours of anger, fear, pain, inflammation and negativity. When pulling out negative energy, I can tell the progress of the release by the intensity and shade of the colour remaining. If the person you are working with is good at sensing or visualising, their feedback on the shades and intensity of the colours will provide insight into the progress and success of the healing work you are doing.

As the healing progresses, it is important to see and sense the negative energy and colours coming out until the energy diminishes and the colours become clear and clean. Then saturate the area with a healing colour. Remember, the more senses you can employ during the healing process, the easier and more profound the healing.

BREATHING

Breathing, essential to living, is also a key indicator of how a person deals with life and how they face their challenges. Few people breathe deeply, rhythmically and in a relaxed manner. Shallow breathing and holding the breath are strong indicators of fear and tension in the body and that a person is stuffing down their pain.

When the person you are working with begins to take shallow breaths or periodically stops breathing, immediately ask them to take a few deep breaths. Encourage them to allow themself to feel whatever is going on, to relax into their feelings and then to breathe into and through the pain.

Visualising while breathing in healing energy and a colour — such as gold, emerald green or pink — can assist in breaking up old patterns, old blockages and any negativity being stored within the body. Breathing into an area of pain or blockage will usually break up the negativity in minutes, when used in combination with healing energy.

INNER CHILD WORK

Our inner child is that part of us which, when healthy, is spontaneous, alive, creative and adventuresome. This inner child is different from the actual child that experienced trauma. This child exists within each of us and is part of the whole person psychologically, emotionally and spiritually. Through visualisation, verbal dialogue, sensing and writing, guided meditation, playing with puppets and drawing pictures we can communicate with our inner child. The information received in this communication can facilitate and speed healing.

In some people the inner child is alive, spontaneous, healthy and well-adjusted. Such people are successful, happy and able to have healthy relationships. This inner child can also communicate with a person; it asks for what it desires and is free to say how it feels. People with a healthy inner child are usually calm, focused and confident.

Those who have experienced a childhood that was traumatic or in which they did not learn healthy interpersonal skills, might have a wounded inner child which is scared and unsure of itself. This adult will usually have trouble functioning in everyday life. Signs of a wounded or hidden inner child are lack of success, unhappiness, inability to have and maintain close relationships and an inability to identify, ask for and obtain what is really desired. Such people tend to be scattered, unfocused and insecure.

To determine the age and health of someone's inner child, ask them to close their eyes, take a few deep breaths and quiet their mind. Then have them ask themself if their inner child is willing to communicate with them. Wait for a 'yes' or 'no' answer. If the answer is 'yes', have them ask it how it feels and what it needs. If the answer is 'no', have them ask it what it needs from them in order to communicate with them. In either case continue your questions in a soft, gentle voice, always thanking them and the child for trusting and communicating.

JOURNAL-KEEPING

Journal-keeping is similar to writing a diary. When you keep a journal you write your thoughts and feelings and explore what is behind them. You also reflect on how your past influences and affects you currently. Journal-keeping is usually done in sequential notebooks so you can go back and review your progress and the changes you have made. The process of sitting down alone in a quiet place and writing privately to and about yourself brings your feelings to the surface so you can experience them more readily. In addition it opens the doorway to allow your deeper subconscious thoughts and feelings to come up to the level of conscious awareness. You are in effect telling your mind, "Yes, I do care, I am listening, please communicate with me." Once you start writing, the words seem to flow, often effortlessly, revealing many pieces of information about yourself that you may not have been aware of before. As you keep your journal, if you write about how you truly feel and then lovingly ask yourself questions, you will usually get some very insightful answers. Writing tends to activate all parts of the brain and draw out the memories and reasons behind the feelings.

Ten

MOVING AND DIRECTING THE ENERGY FLOW

ACTIVELY MOVING THE ENERGY

This procedure works well for a wide variety of illnesses and injuries and is so effective and versatile that it can be used in almost every healing situation.

There are times when it is very important to be able, actively and consciously, to move energy in a precise manner. An excellent way to do this is to direct and focus the energy.

The left hand is the receiver, drawing energy. Use your left hand either to draw negative energy out of a person or to draw positive energy in from the universe. (See Figs. 3 & 4, pp 27 & 28) You can also visualise the left hand as suctioning or vacuuming energy into itself. Use your right hand as your sender, to direct the negative energy that has been pulled out of the person either into the ground or up to the sky to be recycled and transmuted. (See Figs. 3 & 19, pp 27 & 169) You also use your right hand to direct positive healing energy into a person or into a specific area needing healing (see Fig. 4, p 28). This holds true even for people who are left-handed.

Visualise a suction drawing energy into your left hand and through a sealed tube into your body. Remember that you are only a conduit for the energy and keep this energy within the conduit tube. In this way the energy will not enter or affect your body in any way; it will only pass through you. Feel the energy move across your body and come out of your right hand.

When doing healing work on an area of negative energy,

place your left hand 2-6 inches (5-15 cm) above the injured area to draw out the negative energy. Using your right hand, direct the negative energy either up to the sky or down into the earth to be transmuted. Allow the negative energy to drain completely out of the person you are working with. Continue to pull off the negative energy until the flow can no longer be felt. This method can be used to pull concentrated excess energy and pain out of a person, to reduce fever, to withdraw energy from a cancerous tumour or to clear trauma. It works well for all burns, cuts and injuries. After all the negative energy is drawn out of the person, rub or shake your hands to clear off any negative energy that might be clinging to them. Then hold your left palm up in a receiving mode and pull in positive energy from the universe. Positive healing energy is now directed with your right hand into the area to be healed.

Both you and the person you are working with can literally feel the negative energy flowing out of their body. As you do this you will notice that there is a point where the energy decreases until it feels like just a small trickle. Draining the negative energy in a minor injury might take only a few seconds or a few minutes. In the case of serious injuries or illnesses, however, you might have to go back two, three or more times to drain the negative energy completely. It appears that negative energy comes off in layers of different intensities as it is released from the body. When the energy is totally released, the outward flow of negative energy will cease along with almost all sensation of pain.

After the negative energy has stopped flowing, shake and rub your hands together both to clear your own energy and to disconnect and release negative energy. Next tell your hands and the person you are working with that you are now going to put in positive healing energy. You are then ready to put your hands back on the person. With your left palm facing up ask God to send in positive energy.

Ask the person you are working with to visualise receiving the positive energy and a healing colour — emerald green for healing and the heart energy, pink for love, or whatever colour energy they feel they most need in the area to be healed. Ask the person to feel and sense the energy coming to them. Visualise and feel the healing energy being pulled from the universe into your left hand and then being sent out of your right hand into the body. At this point, hold your right hand 2-6 inches (5-15 cm) above the body. As the positive healing energy comes through you, have the person visualise along with you. Together see the affected area being filled completely with the positive healing energy. Fill this area two or three times until it feels like the area is completely healed.

After the area needing healing has been filled with positive energy, the energy coming out of your right hand can be felt slowing down and then stopping just as it did when you were drawing out negative energy. When this energy has stopped, the person has absorbed all the energy that they can possibly take at that time. Rub your hands together again and smooth out the energy field much like icing a cake. Visualise the healing energy being sealed within the person you are working with. Healings can be done as frequently as every few hours in extreme cases. (*NOTE:* In an hour or so the person might be able to absorb more energy. When working with people with serious challenges, multiple treatments are recommended.) For most people, however, one or two sessions are enough.

After this do an aura cleansing above the injured area to smooth out the energy field. With many injuries the energy field around the body is also damaged and traumatised. Whenever a person has had surgery or has been in an accident of any type, it is important to do an aura cleansing to release the trauma, the pain and the energetic memory held in their energy field. By smoothing out the energy field, you are actually mending and reconstructing the rips, tears and abrasions in it. For example, if a person has been cut, the above-mentioned healing processes combined with aura cleansing will remove the negative energy and provide healing energy for both their physical body and their energy field. Visualising healing energy filling the area and positive changes occurring will certainly accelerate the healing process. Focused visualisation is as powerful as the healing energy itself.

ONE vs TWO HANDS

The technique of using one hand is effective in most cases. There are times, however, when you may want to use two hands to send positive energy into the person you are working with. To send positive energy out of both hands, visualise and experience yourself opening the top of your head. Feel healing energy come down through the top of your head to the centre of the earth and back up into your heart. Then feel the healing energy come from your heart and out of both your right and left hands at the same time. By utilising two hands, you can send healing energy to both eyes, ears or kidneys at the same time or to any other area needing attention (see Fig. 14). Focus on allowing energy to come through you and to the person that you are working with. See and feel the energy coming through both of your hands. Visualise the negative energy breaking up, being washed away from the person you are working with and being released into the ground.

TWO HANDS FORMING A TRIANGLE

A simple, effective two-handed method for removing negative energy is the triangle technique. Here, negative energy is neither pulled into your hands nor run through your body. Place your hands palms down, with the tips of your pointer fingers touching and your thumbnails overlapping.

Figure 14 SENDING ENERGY WITH TWO HANDS

Your hands, especially the open area between them, form the shape of a triangle (see Fig. 15).

Form the triangle directly on or 2-6 inches (5-15 cm) above the area to be worked on. Visualise and feel positive energy as well as healing colours coming from the palms of your hands and your fingers, penetrating directly into the area in need of healing. As the positive energy penetrates the area, visualise the negative energy breaking

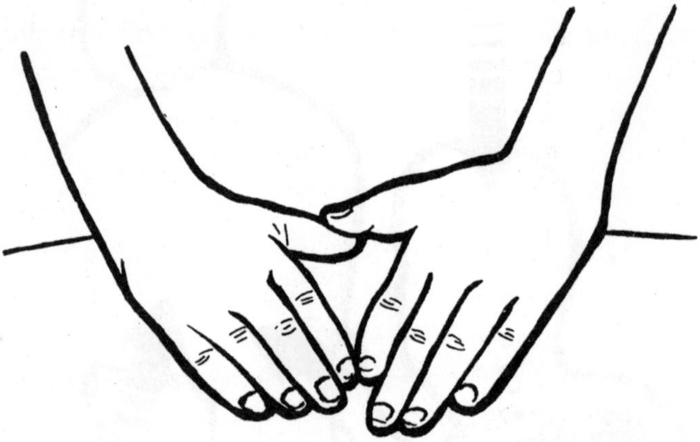

Figure 15 TWO HANDS FORMING A TRIANGLE

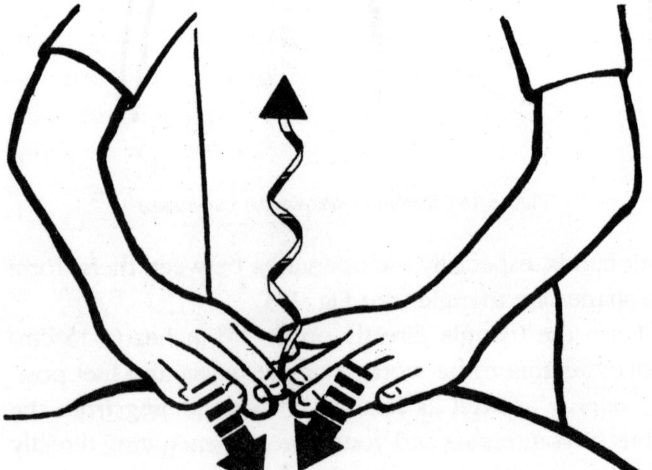

Figure 16 ENERGY MOVEMENT IN TRIANGLE

up. See and feel the negative energy being pushed up and out through the centre of the triangle and being released and immediately transmuted (see Fig. 16). This was the technique used to pull the tumour out of the cat. Please remember to have the person you are assisting visualise the healing process with you.

REACHING IN AND PULLING OUT

Reaching in and pulling out is a technique used to visually and energetically remove tumours, blockages and negative energy within the body. When reaching in and pulling out, hold your right hand, with fingers extended, toward the area to be worked with. With your eyes open or closed, visualise your hand going deep inside the person. See and feel the energy from your hand grasping, locking onto and pulling out the negative energy (see Fig. 17).

For example, in the case of a person who is experiencing throat problems or has a problem verbally expressing themself, hold your right hand 2-6 inches (5-15 cm) from the body with your fingers extended towards their throat. Visualise yourself reaching inside the throat and breaking up, releasing, then pulling out the negative blocked energy.

People confirm that they can actually feel both the healer's hand and the energy moving deep within their body. They can also feel the shifts that occur as a result of the energy unblocking. This technique is excellent for removing specific, identifiable concentrations of negative energy. Remember to have the person you are working with visualise the process with you and give you continuous feedback while you are working.

MOVING BLOCKED ENERGY — SPECIAL TECHNIQUES

In working with negative energy that is difficult to move, seems concentrated or is taking a long time to drain out,

Figure 17 REACHING IN AND PULLING OUT

there are a number of quick, simple techniques that can be used to assist in breaking up these negative energy patterns.

The energy flow may be blocked or sluggish for a variety of reasons. Accumulations of blocked energy can occur in a person who is scared, injured, burnt, hurt, tense or in pain. Regardless of the cause, whenever energy is blocked it can be quite painful.

Power-Pushing — When experiencing very stubborn blocked energy, you can power-push the negative energy out by putting your left hand over the affected area to draw out negative energy and your right hand underneath the place in the body you are working on. Use your right hand to power-push positive energy into the affected area. Visualise this healing energy breaking down the negative energy and pushing it out into your left hand. In effect you are power-boosting the removal of the negative energy. Visualise the energy becoming unblocked and flowing freely. As this negative energy begins to move in the body, see it immediately transmute into positive energy.

This method will force the energy out more quickly than if you are just drawing it out using only your left hand. Before using this two-handed approach try using just the left hand to draw the energy out. If you find that you need an extra boost, use the two-handed technique. Once the energy is unblocked, you can use the one-handed method for drawing out the negative energy.

The following approaches work because the mind cannot hold on to two thoughts at the same time. Here the mind will only hold on to the strongest energy, releasing the weaker one. For example, if you have a headache or pain and then are confronted by a minor crisis, you forget about the headache. *NOTE:* Be aware that your focused intention is required in order for the clapping to shatter the negative energy field.

Inflated Balloon — One approach involves the use of a balloon. Have the person focus on placing the issue they wish to heal into the balloon. Then have them blow these issues into the balloon, filling it as full as possible, and tie it. Have them hold the balloon next to their body over the affected area. Next, with their eyes shut, have the person visualise putting all their emotions — pain, anger, hurt and frustrations — into the balloon. After they have placed all of this in the balloon, tell them that they can release and heal this issue and the related emotions by breaking the balloon. You may even encourage them to get angry at what the issue has cost them and at the pain it has created in their life. Encourage them to let all this anger out by squeezing and breaking the balloon. As they start to squeeze the balloon, watch for a moment when it is being squeezed with a lot of emotion. Then, when the person least expects it, pierce the balloon with a pen or pencil. The noise and the surprise of the balloon's breaking will shatter the negative energy blockage. When you can get the person you are working with to participate actively with you, the healing is always more effective.

Energy Ball — A variation of the above technique is to have the person, with their eyes shut, focus their mind and visualise the energy of their issue or illness. Ask them to gather all of the energy associated with it and to push it out of their body until it is about 12 inches (30 cm) in front of their forehead. Then ask them to compress this energy into a tight ball. After they have done this, ask them again if all of the energy associated with it is out of their body and inside the energy ball. When they say that all of the energy is out of their body, ask them to focus their mind on the energy ball and to compress it even tighter. Wait until you feel that they are totally focused on the energy ball and, when they least expect it, clap your hands as loudly as you can in the area of the energy ball. Usually the energy ball is completely released or, at the least, greatly reduced. If it is only reduced, repeat the process a second or third time, as needed.

Clapping — Another technique is to have the person shut their eyes and focus on the issue they are dealing with. Watch until you can see they have focused intensely on the issue. Then, when least expected, clap your hands as loud as you can in the area of the blockage. Again, this shatters the negative energy. This approach has been used often with great success. *NOTE:* Never clap when a person is integrating healing.

Once I was watching a very experienced and skilled chiropractor work on an individual. The chiropractor adjusted the person's spine in a number of ways; however, no matter what he did, he could not get the energy to flow correctly in the spine. He was about to give up when I asked him if I could try something. He stepped back and, without warning, I clapped my hands as loudly as I could just above the affected area. The doctor checked the spine and was amazed to find that, without any further adjustment, the energy was flowing perfectly.

DETECTING AN ENERGY SHIFT

When an energy release occurs it is perceived as a change or shift in the body's energy. These energy shifts happen whenever a blockage is partially or fully released. They take place on many levels and some are easier to detect than others. When a shift occurs on either the mental, physical or emotional levels, there are certain indicators which give a sensitive healer great insight into the next step to take in assisting the person. Indications of an energy shift can include crying, shaking, yawning, sighs, breath rate changes, taking a deep breath, rolling the eyes, dilation of the pupils, muscle spasms, twitches, burping, passing gas, gurgling intestines, coughing and even laughter. A sharp pain or ache may be an indicator of either an energy release or an area that needs more attention. More subtle indicators of energy shifts are skin colour and body temperature changes. Communicating your awareness of positive shifts to the person receiving the healing provides them with tangible validation that changes within their body have occurred and are continuing to take place.

The ability to identify releases, regardless of the form they take, allows you a much greater insight into both a person's healing process and your own progress. When you have learned how to read these indicators, you can gain valuable information such as how willing and ready a person is to heal or to what extent they are in fear or are stuck.

When the body relaxes completely, it may be a sign that resistance has ended, the blockage has been released and healing is taking place. Although, at least for the time being, the process has been completed, there may be deeper levels to work on at a later date. If you are looking for a stopping point in the session, this may be a good place. Sessions are best ended after a person has completed a process, or if they state that they wish to stop for the day. Avoid ending a session while they are still processing their emotions or are in physical pain. Stopping at this point, without completing the process, will leave the person in an extremely vulnerable position; it is comparable to a doctor's stopping in the middle of surgery without closing the incision.

With a shift on the spiritual level, it might be more difficult to pinpoint a specific time or way the change has occurred. In addition these changes are similar to energy shifts on the mental and emotional levels. They may be indicated by a difference in the skin colouration, by increased aliveness or intensified brightness of the energy field or in the clarity and the brightness of the eyes.

It is important for you to be comfortable with all forms and expressions of release. The greater the level of acceptance, support and unconditional love that you can provide, the safer it will be for a person to open up, to let go of resistance and to release their pain without fear of criticism, judgement or rejection. The clarity and unconditional love you provide will act as a catalyst to heighten the feeling of safety and to encourage a person to face long-hidden issues.

RELEASING EXCESS AND NEGATIVE ENERGY

When doing healing work, there is a possibility that you will accumulate excess energy or pick up negative energy from either the person being worked with, the surroundings or both. It is important that you release this energy after each healing session as quickly and completely as possible.

You can safely release all excess and negative energy in a number of ways. The following is a list of some of the most effective and widely used techniques for clearing energy during a healing session or after you finish working with a person. This energy includes negative energy removed from the person and the surrounding area, as well as any excess energy generated during the session.

1. Physically wash your hands while visualising that you are cleansing and releasing all negative energy from your body.

2. Rub the palms of your hands on the floor or ground, allowing all excess and negative energy to flow out of your body. Visualise this energy being released into the earth to be purified and transmuted.

3. Vigorously shake the energy off your hands or flick it off your fingers, while directing it either down toward the earth to ground it, or up toward the sky to send it back to God to be transmuted.

4. Visualise a filtering screen in the energy flow to trap, burn away and transmute negative energy.

5. Visualise a dumping tube extending from the base of the spine deep into the earth. Create one for yourself and one for the person you are working with. Visualise intense white light flowing through the top of the head and down through the body. See the light breaking up and washing away all negative energy so it can be released from the body and flow down into the earth for transmutation. End the flow only when there is pure white light flowing throughout the tube.

6. Ask for God/Spirit to help you in releasing all excess and negative energy that you may have picked up.

7. Visualise the energy in your workspace as being saturated in intense white light. Continue this visualisation until

the energy is pure.

8. Visualise a violet flame in the healing room burning away and transmuting all negative energy.

9. Visualise a ring of golden light surrounding your healing area preventing any negative energy from spreading outside the ring. Visualise God constantly vacuuming up and transmuting all of the negative energy.

10. Burn a candle — white, gold, pink, green, blue or violet — visualising that it is burning away and transmuting all negative energy.

11. Smudge the area and yourself by burning sage, cedar or sweetgrass. Visualise the smoke burning away and transmuting any negative energy. (Incense can also be used.)

12. Dance or movement is another way of releasing excess and negative energy.

When you allow negative energy to accumulate, you may begin to feel sluggish or heavy. If this occurs, dancing, yoga, meditation, playing tennis or any form of exercise or spiritual practice can be effective for moving the energy in the body, regardless of whether it is your own energy or has come from others.

Remember, taking on another person's pain and pulling their illnesses into your own body will not only fail to help the person you are working with, it will diminish your ability to stay clear.

Always keep your healing area free of negative energy by cleansing it after each session. It is possible for the person you are working with to pick up negative energy from previous healing sessions and to leave feeling worse than when they came in. When you take responsibility for keeping yourself and your work area clear during and after each healing session, you and the people you work with will experience no problems.

Eleven

SPECIFIC HEALING TECHNIQUES

AURA CLEANSING

Aura cleansing is a good technique to use for clearing depression, frustration, pain and sorrow out of a person's energy field. It can also be used to release and smooth out rough or discordant energy that we pick up in the hustle and bustle of everyday living. The auric field can experience holes, tears, bruises, rips and cuts from mental, emotional, physical and spiritual trauma just as the physical body does. An aura cleansing releases and removes blocked or sluggish negative energy from both the auric field and the physical body. As the auric field is cleansed, any denser negative energy in the physical body will partially or completely break up and move into the auric field — where it can be cleared fairly easily. This is why it is important to pay attention to smoothing out the energy field around the body to complete the process of a healing.

Studies indicate that ailments begin to manifest in the auric field long before they become apparent in the physical body (see 'Negative Thought Forms'). Aura cleansing is an effective way to clear out and release negative energy and negative thought forms that could cause illness in the physical body. Many types of undesirable energy, such as fear, trauma, tension and even fever can be released or at least greatly diminished through this method. Aura cleansings are very beneficial for the body and can be used to keep the energy clear and to prevent illness.

An aura cleansing takes only a few minutes and can be done with the person standing up, sitting down (even in a wheel chair) or lying on a bed. The most convenient position is standing up. In extreme cases, for example when working with someone in a hospital bed, you can do an aura cleansing on whichever side of the person is exposed to you. Do not have the person move unless it is absolutely safe for them to do so. In such cases you may not be able to cleanse the aura on all four sides of the body. Know that good results can occur even though only one side of the aura is cleansed.

To do an aura cleansing, first activate the healing energy in your hands. Next visualise your hands becoming large brushes with 2-4 inch (5-10 cm) bristles coming out of your palms. See and feel your hands becoming the brushes, similar to those used on large animals like horses. Know that these brushes can clear all problems, negativity and dark spots from the energy field.

In an aura cleansing always keep your hands 2-6 inches (5-10 cm) away from a person's body and never touch the body. Facing the person you are working with, hold the palms of your hands toward them. Since the auric field extends beyond the physical body, start with your hands about 12 inches (30 cm) higher than the top of the head and parallel to the body (see Fig. 18). Do not hold your hands directly over the top of the head so as not to interfere with the person's connection with their higher self. Bring your hands straight down the entire length of the body, all the way down to the feet, allowing your hands to touch the floor. As you move your hands, visualise the brushes that your hands have become brushing clean and removing any and all negativity from the energy field. As you gain more experience and become more comfortable working with the energy, you can increase the speed at which you move your hands down the body. Remember always to brush the energy from the head down toward the feet. Complete each side, then move clockwise around the person until all four sides have been cleansed.

Notice what you are feeling as you move your hands

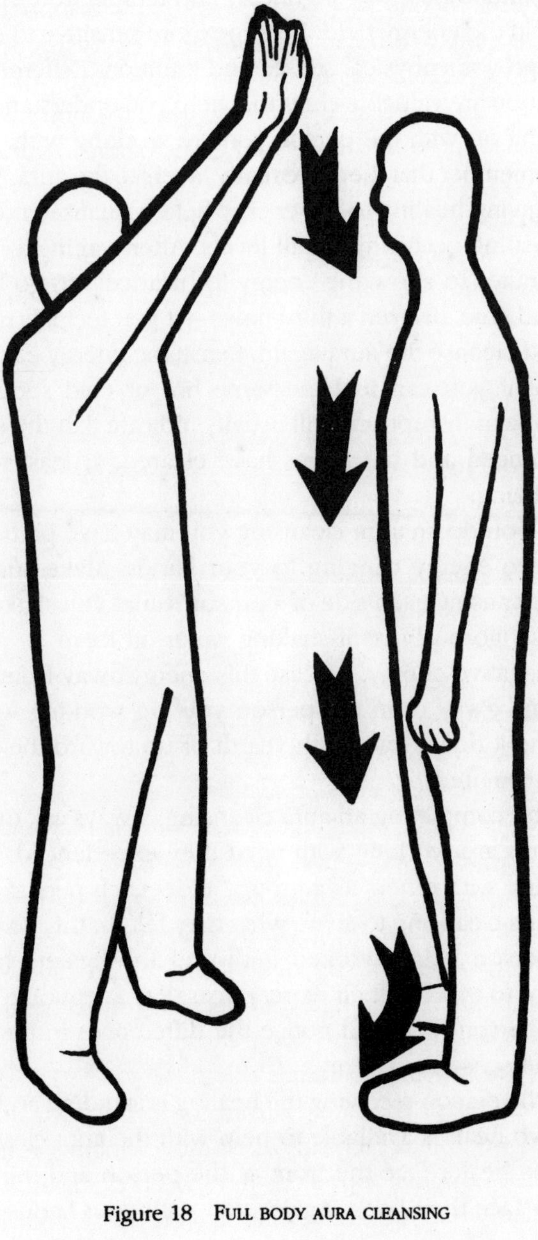

Figure 18 Full body aura cleansing

down the person's body. Be aware of differences in texture (smoothness or roughness) and temperature (heat or cold) in the energy field. Become more sensitive to energy through your physical senses and intuition. Differences in sensation are valuable clues that help you understand what is going on with the person you are working with.

Remember that there are many layers to the aura. Whenever giving healing to the energy field, visualise and sense the healing occurring on all levels. After waiting a couple of minutes to allow the energy to balance out, go back a second time, or even a third time — if you feel it is needed — and cleanse the aura again. Sense the energy each time to see if you can feel the same hot or cold spots. The absence of disruptions will usually indicate that the energy is balanced and blockages have cleared, at least for the time being.

As you do an aura cleansing you may have particles of negative energy clinging to your hands. Make sure that after cleansing each side of a person's aura you shake your hands vigorously, as if shaking water off them, to release any negative energy. Release this energy away from yourself and away from the person you are working with by flicking it down toward the earth or up toward the sky to be transmuted.

After completing an aura cleansing, always ask the person you are working with what they experienced. When working with others as a group, allow each person doing the aura cleansing to share what they felt. In this way both the person being worked with and the healers have a chance to validate their experiences. Pay attention to what each person feels and notice the differences in the ways people sense the energy.

If the person receiving the healing is standing and there are two healers available to help with the aura cleansing, let one healer face the front of the person and the other healer face their back. Again, start with your hands about

12 inches (30 cm) above the person's head and then move your hands slowly to the floor. It works best when both healers synchronise their movements, mirroring each other as they move their hands from head height, to shoulder height, to waist height and the rest of the way down the body. After completing one sweep from head to toe, each healer rotates one quarter turn to the left. Repeat the procedure, cleansing each side of the aura until both healers have cleansed all four sides.

If you have four healers, one faces the front of the person, one the back and one each side. Each healer cleanses their side of the energy field then rotates one quarter turn to the left, until each healer has cleansed all four sides of the energy field.

Almost everyone describes the experience of having their aura cleansed as very refreshing. Many people report that they can actually feel negative energy releases occurring and their energy level increasing and becoming more balanced. Most people feel lighter, more present, alive, awake and clear. Interestingly, the healers doing the cleansing work also report feeling more balanced and relaxed, lighter and freer.

Children and animals have an instinctive desire to be stroked from the head down to the toes. Most children and animals will calm down and lie in your lap quite contentedly when you do this. Even though you are physically touching the child or animal you are, in effect, cleansing their energy field.

You can cleanse your own aura while taking a shower. Visualise the water as white light or healing energy cleansing your auric field. See the negative energy being washed down the drain. This can be done daily or more frequently if desired.

NOTE: To increase or stimulate a person's energy or to make their energy bristle (rather than calming it down), move your hands very quickly *up* their energy field — from the feet to the top of the head. This can be done when a person is sleepy and needs to stay awake. This does not create healing energy; it simply generates large amounts of the type of energy used in physical activity.

WORKING WITH INJURED ARMS OR LEGS

When someone has injured an arm or leg, begin by pulling out the negative energy and putting in positive energy. After completing this, remember that the aura around the person has also been damaged and traumatised. To smooth out the aura around an extremity, position your hands 2-6 inches (5-15 cm) from each side of the arm or leg, starting at the shoulder or hip. With your palms facing the injured area, keep your fingers together and thumbs sticking out from the hand, and smooth out the energy. Smooth the energy away from the body, along the extremity, all the way past the fingers or toes. Bring your hands together 3-6 inches (8-15 cm) beyond the fingers or toes, sealing the energy field. Visualise that you are pulling the negative energy from the auric field (see Fig. 2, p 23 and Fig. 5, p 30).

Remember that trauma and pain are felt in the entire body, not just in the injured area. Because of this it is important to finish the healing by cleansing the entire aura. Again, visualising the healing is as important as smoothing out the energy field. This procedure can be used for any injury involving an arm or leg — such as surgery, a cut, a burn, a stubbed toe, a twisted ankle or a scraped knee.

Here are two examples of foot healings: In the first, a woman had stubbed her toe. As I worked on drawing out the negative energy, she could feel the pain being pulled from her body. The most amazing part of the entire healing was that as I did the aura cleansing she could literally feel the negative energy being pulled from her foot and told me it felt as if I were pulling off a sock by the toe. In the second situation a woman named Shirley was plagued by a sharp foot pain which had bothered her ever since having foot surgery years before. After one of the above treatments the pain left and has never returned.

ENERGY BUILDUP / HEAT ON THE BACK OF THE NECK

An energy buildup experienced as heat on the back of the neck is very common in people who are undergoing major change, passing through a healing crisis or experiencing a rapid increase in spiritual growth. Heat and excess energy might be caused by rapid changes in body chemistry and energy levels. This energy buildup can occur during a change in the relationship between the mind, body and spirit as they rebalance and come into equilibrium and it can cause headaches, tension, frustration and a feeling of being in sensory overload.

The back of the neck is similar to the central processing unit of a computer. All stimuli, messages and responses must flow through this area on their way to and from the brain. This part of the body can easily become overloaded, especially when an overwhelming amount of new information is being received and when rapid changes are occurring.

Close friends of mine have experienced this heat and energy buildup to such an extent that they became disoriented and nauseated and could not function well. In one extreme case I even took my friend Ann out of the city and into the mountains where the trees and fresh air could help ground her.

Going swimming, as well as taking a shower or a bath, can help to drain off excess energy. Taking a hot bath with one cup of either apple cider vinegar or epsom salts added to the bath water will also help.

It is a good idea to check for excess heat on the back of the neck in every person you work with, especially those who are consciously focused on spiritual growth. Once detected, an energy buildup is easy to release. Most people experience relief in seconds.

An easy way to check for heat on the back of the neck is to place the palm of your left hand on, or a few inches behind, the person's neck. Allow yourself to feel the relative temperature and determine whether the neck is hot.

If you detect heat, ask the person to work with you to remove this excess energy. Together, feel and visualise the energy being drained off the neck into your left hand. As you do this, feel this excess energy coming out of your right hand and being sent either down into the earth or up to the sky to be transmuted (see Fig. 19). Continue to drain the energy off until the neck cools. (*NOTE:* In extreme cases clap to release the energy.) Continue with the usual healing procedures.

HEADACHES

Headaches are normally the result of an energy concentration in one part of the brain. This energy buildup, which may be very painful and last for days, can be caused by over-thinking or by attempts to control and/or suppress thoughts and feelings. Headaches commonly occur when the energy in the brain is not flowing smoothly or is overloaded by negative thoughts like fear or anxiety. As soon as this excess energy is removed, or the person changes their thinking process, the headache normally will disappear quickly, leaving the person calmer and more relaxed. Most headaches, even severe ones, can be relieved within a few minutes. However, if the person does not choose to change their thinking patterns, or is resisting experiencing their thoughts and feelings, they may re-create the headache within a short time.

Clearing and removing headaches requires the use of a specific type of aura cleansing. Have the person sit in a chair with their back you. Activate the healing energy in

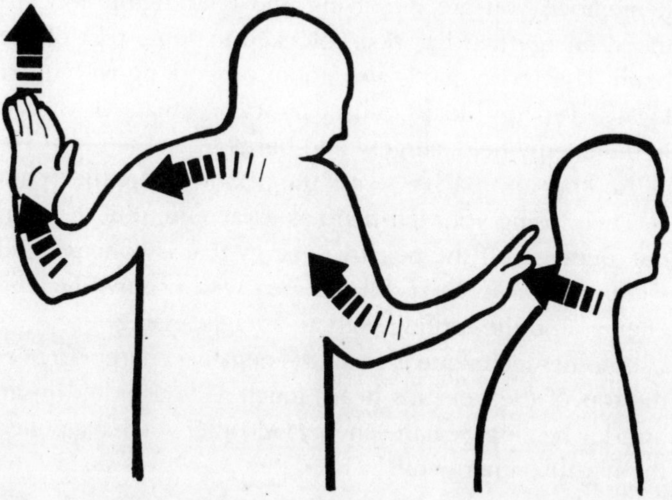

Figure 19 Removing heat on the back of the neck

your hands. Begin with the previously described aura cleansing technique around the head area only. Next, imagine the person's head is a spherical cake and the energy field around their head is the icing. The objective is to frost the cake, distributing the icing evenly in a random swirling pattern. Visualise your hands as spatulas and position them 2-6 inches (5-15 cm) from the head. Randomly move your hands left to right, up and down, and in circular patterns, smoothing out and distributing the energy evenly all around the head. Allow your intuition to show you what you need to do to release the excess energy. It really doesn't make any difference what the sequence is. Smooth the energy out over the entire head and neck, front to back, top to bottom, side to side. Smoothing out the energy will help remove the negative energy from the person's head and auric field. You will know when you have unblocked the energy because the person's headache will disappear. Remember, you are dissolving and rearranging concentrated energy that has been blocked in some part of the brain. This technique is also good for working with other localised energy blocks, caused by scars, damage or a break in the energy field, surgery and burns.

Another approach is to ask the person where their pain is. Then, using your left hand as a vacuum, pull the pain out, drawing off the negative energy that is concentrated within that area. Next, fill the area with positive healing energy. End the healing with an aura cleansing.

Another technique is to lift the negative energy up over the top of the person's head, much as you would in an arm/leg healing. Seal the energy field after you have pulled the negative energy off.

BALANCING RIGHT/LEFT BRAIN

Balancing the right and left brain is especially beneficial for people who operate more from one side of their brain than the other. Artists and musicians tend to be right brain dominant; engineers and mathematicians tend to be left brain dominant. Balancing helps increase the flow of energy between the two hemispheres of the brain and thereby helps the brain to operate as a whole rather than depending heavily on either the right or left half. Balancing can assist in eliminating headaches and stress, and helps a person stay centred and grounded and maintain an internal balance.

A good way to balance the right and the left brain is to have the person you are working with sit in a chair. Stand behind them, facing their back. If they cannot sit down, have them lie down in front of you, with the top of their head toward you. Rub your hands together to activate the energy and place them near each side of the head. Keep the palms of your hands positioned 2-6 inches (5-15 cm)

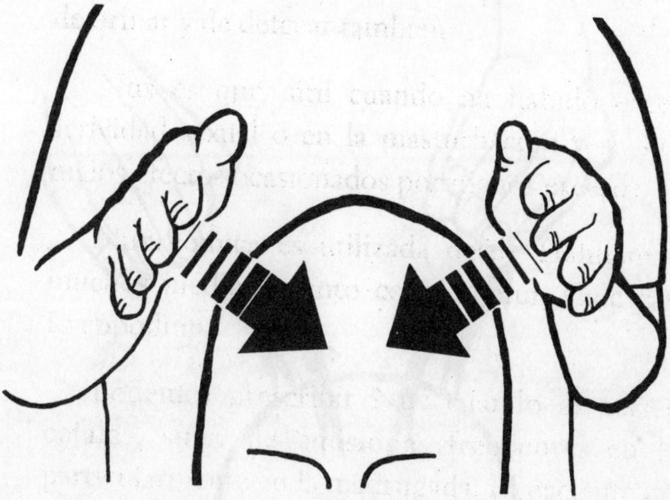

Figure 20 BALANCING RIGHT AND LEFT BRAIN

out from the side of the head, just above the ears. Now send healing energy out of both your hands (see Fig. 20). The energy will flow through both sides of the brain, blending and balancing the energy level of each side. As the healing energy flows into the centre of the brain, visualise any negative energy being instantly transmuted. Allow energy to flow through your hands for 2-5 minutes, or until the energy flow either feels equally balanced or stops.

CLEARING THE CROWN CHAKRA

When balancing the chakras always start with the crown chakra and work down the body on each chakra in sequence. Cleansing and balancing the crown chakra utilises healing techniques very different from the others

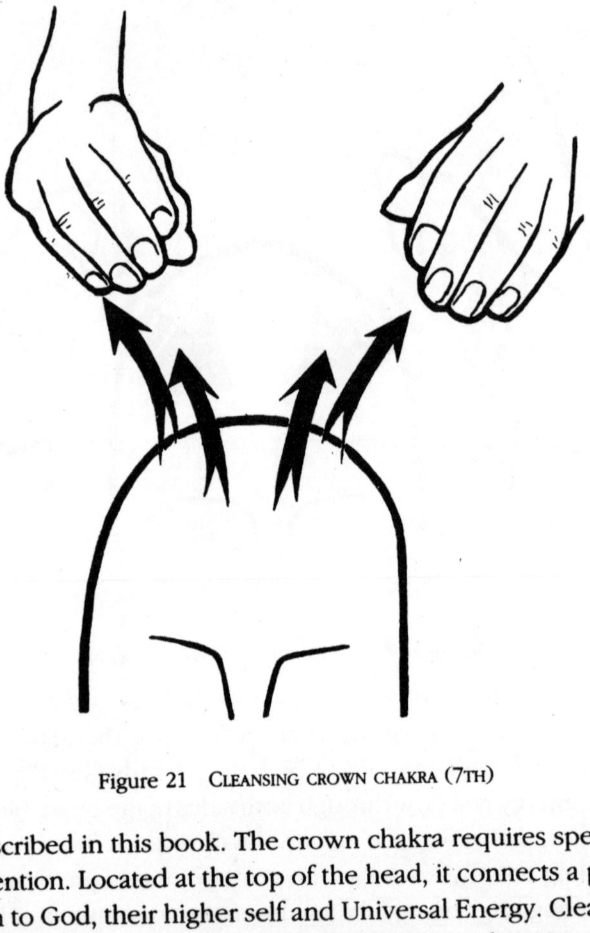

Figure 21 CLEANSING CROWN CHAKRA (7TH)

described in this book. The crown chakra requires special attention. Located at the top of the head, it connects a person to God, their higher self and Universal Energy. Cleansing the crown chakra assists the person in keeping this connection clear. It allows greater insight and clearer guidance, reduces confusion and increases clarity.

To cleanse the crown chakra, visualise the top of the person's head as a garden with a 4-inch (10-cm) pillar of light extending upward from the centre. Visualise weeding this garden while moving your hands to remove any negative energy (the weeds). Work around the edge of the pillar of light — *not* directly in it (see Fig. 21). Stop when

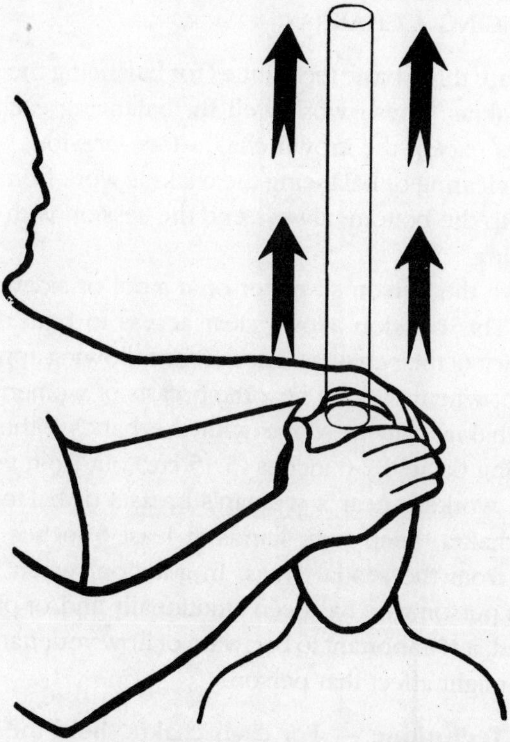

Figure 22 CLEANSING CROWN CHAKRA (7TH).

you feel that the cleansing (weeding) is complete.

Visualise or sense the pillar of intense white or golden energy connecting the person to God/Holy Spirit. Using the aura cleansing technique, clear the energy of this pillar just as you would clear the aura around the body. Position your hands as if you were gently holding the base of this 4-inch (10-cm) pillar, next to the head. Starting at the base of the pillar, move your hands up the pillar until you reach about 36 inches (1 m) above the person's head (see Fig. 22). See or sense the negative energy clearing. Repeat this three times or until the energy is clear. Continue to cleanse the other chakras and end with an aura cleansing.

BALANCING A CHAKRA

There are three basic techniques for balancing the remaining chakras. These work well for balancing each of the chakras except the crown chakra (see previous section). When clearing or balancing the chakras work from the top down to the bottom; always end the session with an aura cleansing.

Have the person sit either on a stool or sideways in a chair. This position allows clear access to both the front and back of their chakras. Each of the following approaches (except when working near the breasts of women and the root chakra) can be done with the hands either gently touching or held 2-6 inches (5-15 cm) out from the body. When working near a woman's breasts or balancing the root chakra, keep your hands at least 6 inches (15 cm) away from the sexual areas. In addition, when working with a person who has been emotionally and/or physically abused, it is important to be aware of how your hand placement might affect that person.

First Technique — For each chakra, hold the palm of your right hand on the centre of the spine behind the area you are working with, sending positive healing energy into the area. At the same time hold your left hand in front of the body to draw out any pain or negative energy. Experience the positive healing energy going from your right palm through the person and circulating back around again and again, breaking up any blockages and clearing out any negative energy patterns. Visualise a filtering screen in the energy flow outside the body. This screen traps and instantaneously burns off and transmutes any and all negative energy being released. Continue to do this until the energy is clear; always end the session with an aura cleansing.

Second Technique — Visualise healing energy coming out of both your hands at once and meeting in the middle of the chakra. Visualise and feel the energy and healing colours in the centre of the chakra, blessing, cleansing and purifying it. Visualise and sense all negative energy simply melting away and being instantly transmuted.

Third Technique — As needed: (1) Use the left hand to draw off negative energy, then use the right hand to fill the area with positive energy, (2) reach in and pull out, (3) clap, (4) use the balloon technique. Always end with an aura cleansing.

People have reported feeling a vibration in their chakras, a shift in their energy, a tingling, warmth or a gurgling sensation. Many experience a release as healing energy moves through and fills the chakras. Most people carry emotional pain from past experiences, relationships and disappointments. By using these simple techniques you can assist a person in releasing the pain of past experiences and help them to heal. It is not unusual for people to cry openly or for tears to well up during this process.

Chakra	Hand placement	Fig.
6th	Right — lower third of back of head Left — front of forehead	23
5th	Right — back of neck Left — front of throat	24
4th	Right — behind heart Left — front of heart	25
3rd	Right — behind base of sternum Left — front of base of sternum	26
2nd	Right — back of navel/spleen Left — front of navel/spleen	27
1st	Right — behind base of spine Left — in front of sexual organs	28

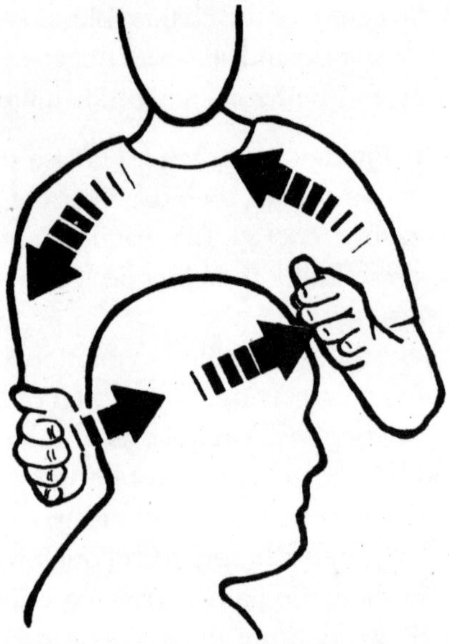

Figure 23 CLEANSING THIRD EYE CHAKRA (6TH)
Right hand: lower third of back of head. Left hand: front of forehead.

Figure 24 CLEANSING THROAT CHAKRA (5TH)
Right hand: back of neck. Left hand: front of throat.

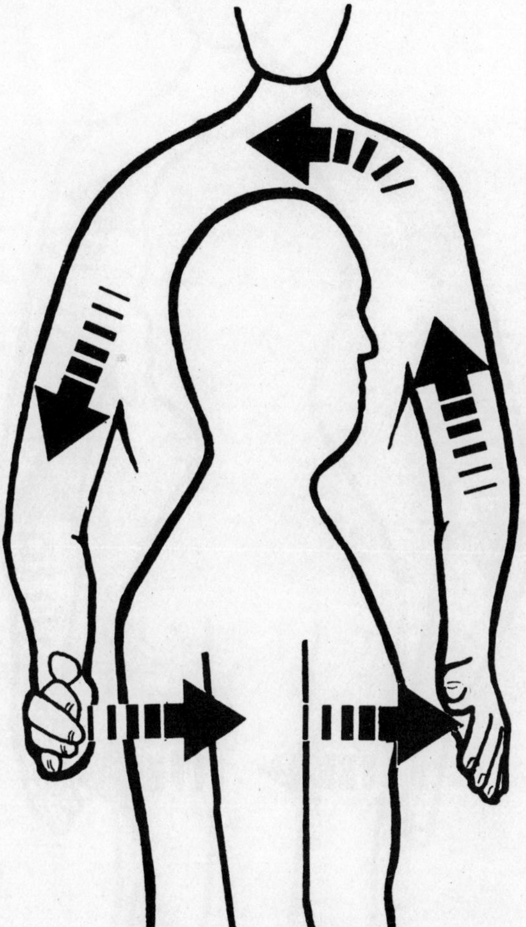

Figure 25 CLEANSING HEART CHAKRA (4TH)
Right hand: behind heart. Left hand: front of heart

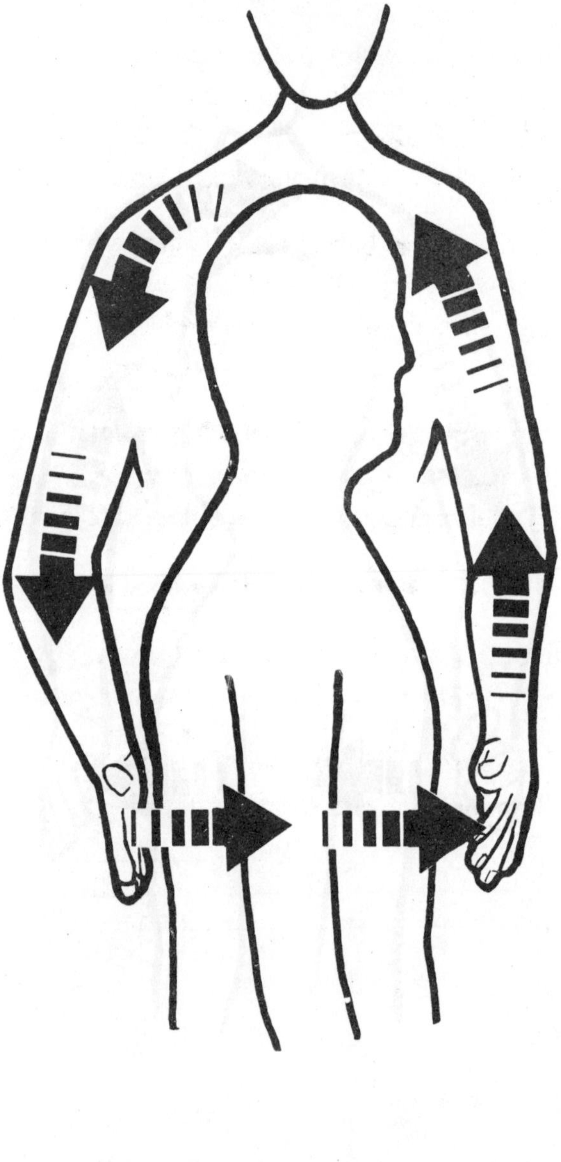

Figure 26 CLEANSING SOLAR PLEXUS CHAKRA (3RD)
Right hand: behind base of sternum. Left hand: front of base of sternum

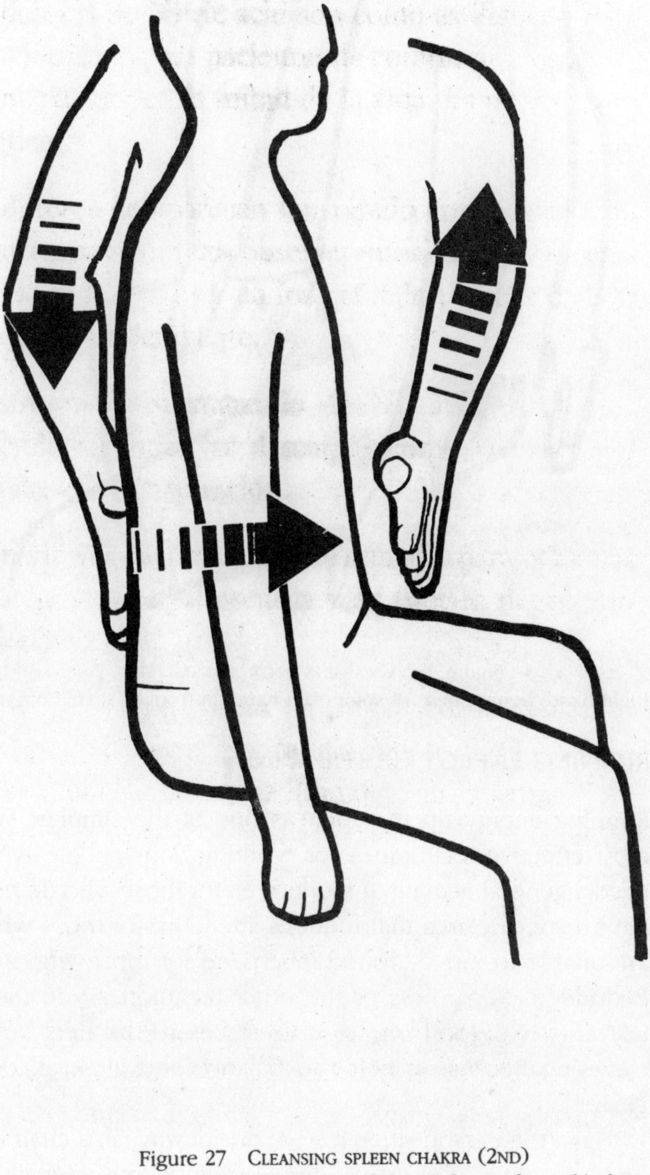

Figure 27 CLEANSING SPLEEN CHAKRA (2ND)
Right hand: back of navel/spleen. Left hand: front of navel/spleen

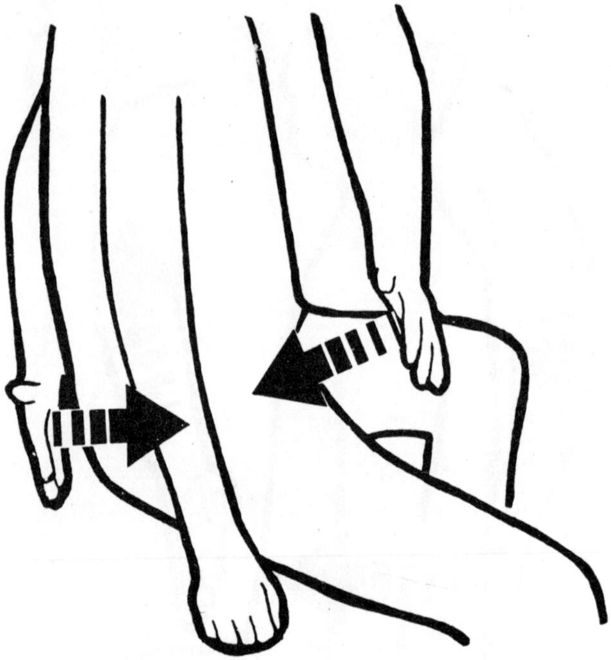

Figure 28 CLEANSING ROOT CHAKRA (1ST)
Right hand: behind base of spine. Left hand: in front of sexual organs

RUNNING ENERGY UP THE SPINE

Running energy up the spine is one of the simplest yet most effective techniques for working with people who need a general healing. It works well for those who do not have a specific area that requires attention, for those who are unable to move around much and for those who are bedridden. Regardless of the other techniques you may use, this is a good one to do just before the final aura cleansing because it helps to balance and align all the chakras.

Have the person sit on a stool or sideways in a chair or lie face down. After activating your hands, put your right

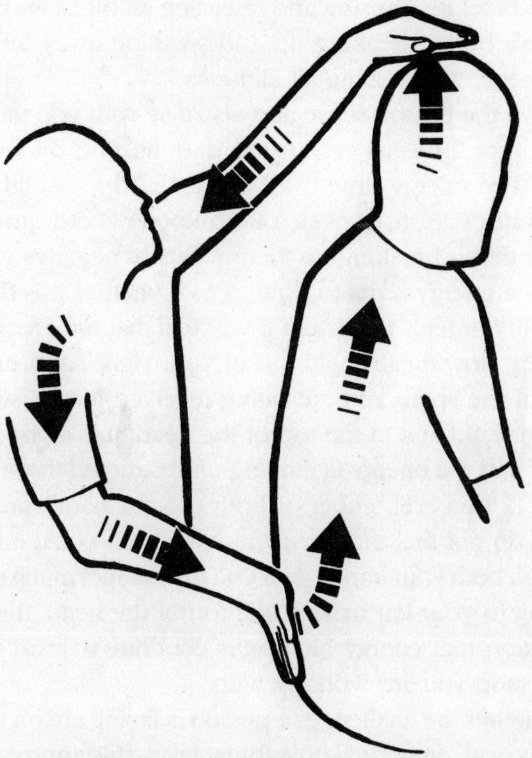

Figure 29 RUNNING ENERGY UP THE SPINE

palm at the base of their spine and your left palm facing downward 2-6 inches (5-15 cm) above the top of their head (see Fig. 29). Ask the person to join you in sensing or visualising the energy moving out of your right hand into the base of their spine and then running up from the base of their spine and out the top of their head into your left hand. Visualise the energy circulating back from the top of their head to the base of their spine, forming a continuous energy loop through and around their body. Visualise a filtering screen in the energy flow outside the body — as it moves back to the base of the spine. This screen traps and instantaneously burns away or transmutes any negative energy in the flow. Continue to circulate this energy. As it circulates, see and feel it cleansing and releasing all blockages in the person's body, breaking up and washing away all negative energy and healing all ailments.

Have the person sense and visualise with you the healing energy blessing, cleansing and healing all blocked areas. The energy flow can be visualised as a high-pressure water stream, or even a Roto-Rooter (Rotovator) type of tool that is breaking up the pockets of negative energy.

Once energy starts to flow, sense whether it is flowing smoothly or feels restricted. If you feel that the energy and heat are flowing strongly out of your right hand into the base of the spine and are being received just as strongly by your left hand at the top of the head, it is a good indication that the energy is moving unobstructed through the body. If, however, either or both of your hands are cold, if you do not feel the energy moving with equal intensity through both your hands, or if you cannot feel much energy coming to your left hand at the top of the head, this is an indication that energy blockages continue to exist within the person you are working with.

Whether the challenges a person is facing are on a mental, physical, emotional or spiritual level, this approach will assist to calm them, balance their overall energy and help their energy to flow more effectively.

It is typical for someone to relate that they are feeling tingling heat moving up the spine or that they can feel the energy moving through certain places in their body. This technique allows the energy to go where it is most needed. If there are any blockages or areas where the energy is not flowing smoothly within the body, this technique will help to loosen and unblock the energy and then move it out of the body. It can be used whenever someone's energy is low and is effective for all types of illness, regardless of cause or severity — even cancer and AIDS.

Because this technique is simple and beneficial, it is a very good one to practise with. Allow yourself to sense the energy, and be aware of what you are feeling. Be sure to ask the person you are working with what they are feeling, so that you can get feedback on their experience.

SEALING THE AURIC FIELD

Sealing the auric field is done after the aura has been cleansed. The sealing process creates a protective shield which fits tightly around the energy field, insulating it from negative energy. It is important to do this whenever a person is feeling fragile or does not have time to relax after a healing session or especially if they are going out into a high-stress or hectic environment. Although a healing session and aura cleansing clear out negative energy, a person can be sensitive, open and vulnerable to the negative energy of other people or a stressful environment, especially if a major release has occurred.

To seal the auric field, have the person stand facing you. Because you are working in their energy field keep your hands 2-12 inches (5-30 cm) out from the body. Extend your hands upward at a 45 degree angle, at least 12 inches (30 cm) above and beyond the body (see Fig. 30). Move your hands in a fluid motion at a 30-45 degree angle down toward the centre of the body; cross the centre and continue at a 30-45 degree angle to the opposite side. When your hands reach the opposite side move them diagonally back to the original side of the body, again crossing at the centre. Repeat this movement until you reach the floor. Your hand movements will resemble the outline of figure 8s stacked vertically on top of one another.

As you are moving your hands, visualise the energy field condensing and becoming more compact and sealed, actually forming a skin-tight protective energy shield around the person. Seal the auric field from head to foot on each of the four sides of the body just as you cleansed the auric field on all four sides. Move consecutively from one side

Figure 30 SEALING THE AURIC FIELD

to the next in a clockwise direction. People who have had their aura sealed have described themselves as feeling smaller, or as if they were in a tight bodysuit. In almost all instances, they felt very much protected and very safe.

MIND-TO-MIND HEALING

Mind-to-mind healing is accomplished by visualising and focusing the mind and uses all of the same techniques and approaches as hands-on healing, only without the physical use of the hands. With mind-to-mind healing physical contact or proximity is not necessary, which allows you to assist people you might not otherwise have been able to help because of social setting or physical distance.

This technique works well when assisting people in hospital intensive care units or in other public places where the use of hands-on healing might be considered inappropriate. It is also useful when a person cannot be physically approached or touched.

Mind-to-mind healing can be done whether the person receiving the healing energy is physically present or not. If the person is present, you can, with your eyes open or closed, visualise yourself doing the healing techniques, without ever physically moving or touching the person. Normally it is easier to do the healing with your eyes closed because it eliminates distraction and enables your mind to focus better. This technique is equally effective when the person receiving the healing energy is not physically in the same room as the healer. The healing will occur regardless of whether or not you are able to see the person or have physical contact with them.

ETHICS OF ABSENTEE HEALING

When a person asks for a healing or for help for themself, it is obvious that they are personally asking for help. I call this a direct, personal request. Whenever I have a clear request I ask the person what I can do to assist them. Many times, however, a friend or member of the family calls, asking for help for another individual. Here a clear request from the person to be worked on has not been received.

At no time do I ever send an absentee healing without first finding out if the person desires assistance. Many times, my guides or teachers have told me that I am to back off and allow others to have their pain until they ask for help. Once they ask, verbally or through their actions, I am free to assist them.

Too many times, people have been violated by those with good intentions but with little respect for another person's process. Imposing your will to heal someone over that person's will is no different from a group waging a religious war to try to convert others. In my experience, if you try to push healing energy into someone who isn't ready or willing, that person will reject the energy and little, if any, good will result.

Before starting an absentee healing of someone who has not personally asked for help, I quiet my mind and go inside to ask if it is appropriate for me to work with this person. Usually I will get a clear 'yes' or 'no' answer from within myself. Another approach is to visualise or sense the person, or their energy, in my mind's eye and ask if I have permission to assist them. Again, I will usually get a 'yes' or 'no' answer, or at least a feeling one way or the other.

In all cases where I am unsure of the person's openness to or desire for assistance, or where I receive no clear answer, I will not send healing energy to the person's body or their energy field. What I will do, however, is sense and visualise a large ball of intense healing energy within easy reach of the person. This large ball of swirling, healing energy contains a very high energy mass with all of the healing colours: gold, violet, white, pink and emerald green. In this way, I allow the person to choose whether to accept the healing energy and am not in any way imposing my will or the healing energy upon them. For example: You are driving past an auto accident where medical help has already arrived. You may wish to help yet cannot or feel it would be inappropriate to stop. Mind-to-mind healing can be used to send calming energy (pink or white light) or healing energy (emerald green light) to the people involved.

Another approach, which can be used separately or in combination with sending the ball of healing energy, is to pray for God, Holy Spirit or the most appropriate healing angels to work with the person to assist in their healing. In this way, I stay totally out of the picture, and do not in any way violate a person's space, beliefs or energy field.

LONG-DISTANCE HEALING

Long-distance healing is identical to mind-to-mind healing except that the visualisation and healing process is done over longer distances. In long-distance healing the person can be hundreds or even thousands of miles away and still experience the full benefits of the healing. The actual physical distance is not a factor.

For me, the most amazing part of long-distance healing is that healing takes place even though you may not know the person's full name, exact location, age or specific ailment. All that is required for you to help a person is to be able to associate with their energy somehow — through a photograph, a first or last name, some minor detail or piece of information about them, or a combination of the above.

When I am in direct communication with the person I am working with, we agree on a time when we can both relax and focus on the healing. During the healing, I sit down, relax, close my eyes and focus my energy. I sense and visualise the person, seeing both their physical body and their auric field, then work with them in my mind just as I would if they were physically in front of me.

When I am not in direct communication with the person I am working with, I do my best to choose a time when they are most likely to be either asleep or resting. The more relaxed a person is, the easier it is for them to accept the healing energy. The person may or may not be consciously aware that healing energy has been sent to them.

In many instances, the person receiving the healing energy notices a change in the way they are feeling at the time that the healing is sent. People have even called me, accurately reporting the times I have worked with them. They could even describe what had been done, and shared how much better they felt afterwards. Once again, this confirms the power of your mind and of your thoughts. When your mind and your thoughts are focused, you can achieve incredible results.

BLESSING FOOD

You can send energy into food to bless and energise it, and to remove impurities. By blessing and energising your food, you are increasing the food's life force energy. This extra energy is then available to nourish and nurture your body. Removing harmful chemicals, pesticides and other toxins before they enter your body allows it to be healthier and to function more efficiently.

To bless the food and remove impurities, place it in front of you. First, say a prayer and rub your hands together to activate the energy. Then place your hands facing each side of the food, or slightly over it, at about a 45 degree angle. Visualise and feel the energy coming out of the palms of your hands into the food, blessing and cleansing it. In addition to the energy, visualise the vivid colours of healing energy being sent into the food. See any and all impurities being transmuted and released, floating upward through the space between your hands or downward through your body into the earth.

As I do this, I can actually sense and feel the impurities being released. It is surprising to realise the level of impurities in almost all the food you eat. Blessing and energising the food greatly assists your body in self-healing.

BLESSING YOURSELF

Something that is good for everyone, and can be done for the self, is blessing yourself. I have found this technique to be extremely helpful, quick and effective.

Say an opening prayer and then activate your hands. Hold your left palm up to receive energy from the universe and position your right palm facing downward 2-6 inches (5-15 cm) above your own head. Visualise and sense positive energy — white or golden light — being pulled into your left hand and then being sent out from your right hand, down through the top of your head, down through your body, flowing out from the base of your spine and the bottoms of your feet, all the way to the centre of the earth (see Fig. 31). See and feel the positive energy break up and wash away any and all negativity that may exist in your mind and body. Experience the positive energy cleansing, purifying and blessing your entire body. Feel this energy washing over and through you like a waterfall, cleansing you completely and filling you with positive white light, golden energy and unconditional love. This visualisation can also be done while taking a shower. This is an excellent technique for centring and balancing yourself.

PRAYER LISTS

Many churches and organisations have prayer lists, prayer/healing circles and prayer vigils where people may attend or call in and ask that prayers be said for themselves or for

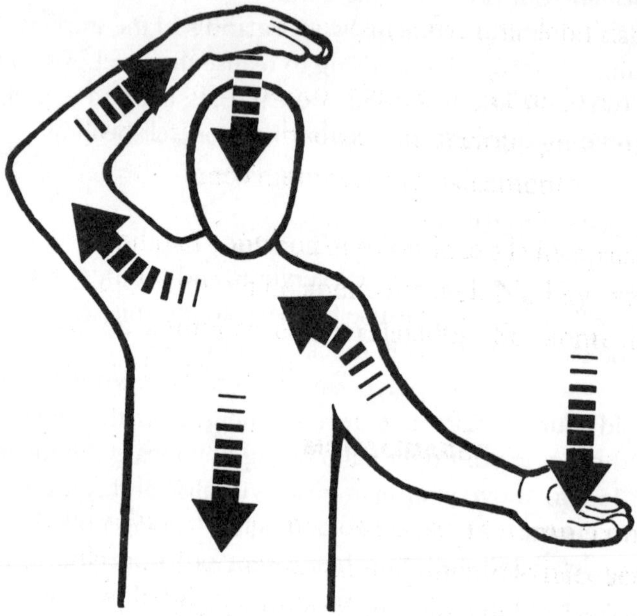

Figure 31 BLESSING YOURSELF

someone they know. The Church of Religious Science, Unity Church and many other religious groups offer this service.

I have found that attending a circle or calling in and asking to be placed on these prayer lists is an extremely powerful source of healing and reinforcement. I highly recommend that anyone in need of help and support, especially those in crisis, take advantage of this excellent source of healing.

It is not important that you be a member of these churches or organisations, or even be known by the members who may be praying for you. Many times, I have called several of the churches around the country to obtain support for myself or loved ones in times of crisis. The results have always been excellent.

PLANETARY HEALING

Using a combination of visualisation, creative intention and long-distance healing, healing energy and healing colours can be sent anywhere in the universe. This energy can be directed to the entire universe at once or to a specific person or place.

General areas needing healing might include the attitudes of all world leaders, members of a peace negotiating team, the children of the planet, the plant kingdom or the ozone layer. The ending of all wars and the visualisation of world peace is one of our highest priorities. Specific areas might include a world leader with a health challenge, a city ravaged by an earthquake or a volcano about to erupt.

When sending planetary healing, focus on visualising and sensing the positive end result and let the 'Universal Intelligence' handle the details of how it will come about. You can also send healing energy and healing colours without visualising a specific outcome. With either approach trust 'creative intention' to guide the healing energy to where it is most needed. Please be sure to pray that all energy sent be for 'the highest good of all concerned'.

Groups have formed worldwide to send healing energy and healing colours for planetary healing. These groups whether small (2-5 people) or large (ten people or more) are having a major positive impact on our universe. Obviously the larger the group and the more focused they are, the greater the potential energy field. Please be aware that even one individual alone sending healing energy to the planet is making more of a difference than they can ever imagine.

Many of the positive changes now being experienced on the planet are the direct result of the healing energy being sent. For example, some cities have reported much lower crime rates when groups meditated and sent healing energy.

One of the methods to send healing energy to the planet is exactly the same as for blessing food. Instead of a plate of food, imagine that a miniature Earth is in front of you. Close your eyes and hold your hands with palms facing the Earth and send healing energy to it. Imagine the negativity melting away. Another method of sending healing is to relax in a chair and use the long-distance healing technique to send healing energy to the planet.

Please spend at least 15 minutes each day, as a tithe to the universe, sending out healing energy and meditating on world peace. This is a great way to develop your healing skills while being of service to the planet.

Twelve

THE HEALING SESSION

PREPARING FOR A HEALING SESSION

When preparing a room for a healing session do your best to have a towel, wastebasket, tissues, pillow and blanket on hand. These are seldom available when working with people in spontaneous situations.

There are many ways to express and release strong emotions safely. I do my best to keep the towel or pillow handy, just in case the person needs to scream. With a towel or pillow over their mouth a person can scream, even at the top of their lungs, without fear of embarrassment or of someone calling the police. Many times these screams will come out uncontrollably, without warning, and there is not time even to reach for the towel. In all cases, I just do my best.

The pillow can be used to hold like a teddy bear for comfort, to cry into, yell into or to punch. Once again, have the person focus their emotions on an external object rather than on you, themself or an inappropriate object that they might hurt or be hurt by. Tissues are kept close to be given for wiping off tears or for blowing the nose. It is best to give tissues after the healing and not during, unless the person specifically asks for them. The reason for this is that if you give them the tissues during their process, you may pull them out of their feelings before they have finished their process. (See 'Supporting the Healing Process'.)

The blanket is kept handy in case the person becomes cold or is chilled during an energy release. The wastebasket is a precaution just in case the person needs to throw up.

CREATING A SAFE ENVIRONMENT

Knowing how to create a safe environment is as important as knowing how to work with the healing energy. Few, if any, of us were raised in an environment of unconditional love and safety. Hence, we have all learned how to guard and insulate ourselves. As we were growing up, these layers of insulation served to keep us alive and from feeling our pain. Over time we have built up layer upon layer of protection. Creating a safe environment assists in removing these layers more quickly.

For people to heal, they must feel safe enough to drop their guard, to face their issues, to feel their feelings and to release the energy associated with their pain, fears and trauma. The less people feel judged, criticised or condemned by others, the more easily they can relax their own self-judgement, self-criticism and self-condemnation, and begin to accept themselves. With this, the healing process becomes easier.

I have done my best to work with people in a private, quiet setting whenever possible; however, at times this is impossible. One time I worked with someone in the main hallway of a hospital. The setting is important, but more important is the level of unconditional love, trust and acceptance that you as a healer bring to the environment.

All of the techniques described in this book are used with a person fully dressed. There have been times when someone has been wearing a coat or a heavy sweater in addition to a shirt and I have asked them if they would be comfortable taking off the heavy outer garment. This is appropriate. Asking someone to disrobe totally is neither necessary nor appropriate.

Confidentiality is also extremely important. Whatever someone says or does during a healing session is strictly confidential and any discussion with others of the person's name or issues is a breach of trust. This will not only have a negative impact on the trust and healing of the person concerned, but can also destroy the reputation of the healer within his or her community. Confidentiality is very important indeed.

HEALING — SETTING THE ENERGY

It is extremely important that you release, or at least set aside, all of your personal problems, issues and challenges before doing any kind of healing work on another person. It is also imperative that you release any judgements you might have about the person you are to work with or the issues they are dealing with.

Your personal life experiences may be shared sparingly, and only when appropriate. Remember that as a healer you are there to assist the person you are working with — they are not there to listen to your problems, nor to heal you. As you work with others you automatically stir up your own unresolved issues. These must be resolved at a time other than during someone else's healing session.

Be as calm, relaxed and unrushed as possible. People who have been abused are extremely vulnerable and sensitive. Much of healing is about helping people to open up and unmask their vulnerability. If they feel rushed or pushed in any way, it may only scare them, causing them to withdraw or shut down even more.

Proceed at a pace comfortable to the person you are working with. If in doubt, it is always better to work at a pace slightly slower than they can handle rather than take a chance on overwhelming them. When someone is overloaded, or even starts to feel that way, they can use it as an excuse to give up, shut down and run away.

Some time ago I did energy work with a woman for only 10 minutes and spent about an hour just talking with her. She pushed for me to do more energy work. However, something inside me said 'no'. Initially she was very upset with me, but later in the week she told me that the work we had done was so powerful that she was barely able to function at work. Ten minutes had been almost too much!

In creating a safe space, first free yourself of all judgement, criticism or preconceived ideas. I have counselled murderers and rapists, as well as survivors of similar crimes. I also have worked with people who have lost loved ones and with both men and women who have been emotionally and sexually abused. All need and deserve healing! All need and deserve forgiveness and a chance to heal their pain. We cannot help another person when we sit in judgement! Remember, God doesn't condemn or judge — only humans persecute one another!

Stay totally present; focus your mind and your full attention on the person you are working with. Look them in the eyes as they share their story. Be there for them and let them know that you hear them — really hear them — and love and support them unconditionally.

If outside thoughts enter your mind, allow them to pass through. A good way to stay present is to practise repeating to yourself the last five words the person has said.

Listen, listen, listen. I have learned that in most cases a person will tell you, or at least give you very strong clues, about both the nature of their problems and the path through which they will accept healing. Active listening — listening to what is not being said as well as what is being said — is an extremely helpful tool.

Accept people where they are. It is almost impossible for people to change until they can accept themselves as they are. For centuries we have been made wrong for every reason under the sun. Unfortunately we are used to being made wrong. Sometimes we just expect it. Other times we actually create being wrong to get negative attention.

What happens, then, when we are made right? What happens if someone is told, "Yes, I can see how you got where you are. It makes sense that you are there." And then if they are asked, "Would you like to change it?" "What would you like to do differently?" "When would you like to experience this change?" "Would you like some help?" After answering these questions, a person is usually able and willing to move forward, not from a place of shame but from a place of personal power.

Ask questions, offer suggestions and avoid 'shoulds'. Asking questions allows the person you are working with to get in touch with their own inner knowing. When you gently ask questions you open doorways that a person didn't even know existed in themself. Ask a question and be still, remaining quiet so the person can go inside and get their own answer.

In many cultures the spiritual leaders teach not by giving answers but by asking questions. Leading questions — such as, "Do you think more exercise would help you to feel better? Or more rest? Or changing this or that in your life?" — can be very useful in helping a person to find their own answers.

At all costs avoid telling someone what you think they 'should' do. 'Shoulding' is merely an imposition of your own ideas, values and judgements onto another person. In most cases, their problems began by listening to someone else's 'shoulds'. Yours can only complicate the situation.

People pick up, through the subconscious or other senses, everything that the healer is thinking and feeling. Although the person may not be able to verbalise clearly what they are picking up or specifically identify where they are getting their impressions from, they will still feel them. For this reason it is extremely important to be as present and as clear as possible with everyone you work with.

When working with some people, fast movement or loud noises may scare or startle them. So move slowly and deliberately, especially with someone who has been beaten or abused. Remember, creating safety is a vital key to successful healings.

SUPPORTING THE HEALING PROCESS

Many times — while a person is telling you what they feel or is crying — you may want to hug them, touch them or give them tissues. If you jump in to comfort someone who is crying or otherwise releasing emotions, you may interrupt or halt their healing process. Once this has happened, it is very difficult for the person to reconnect with their feelings, causing them to lose a golden opportunity to heal.

Often I have seen someone in deep process, crying almost hysterically, being offered tissues. I have watched in total disbelief as the person receiving the tissues came out of their feelings, out of their process, stopped crying and then — in a very calm and centred voice — thanked the person for the tissues. This is only one example of how someone's process can be interrupted or stopped. Allowing a person to go fully into their feelings and experience their pain and trauma permits them to release their energy blockages. Feeling all of one's feelings is one of the quickest roads to healing. Allow a person to stay in their process!

When I see people reaching out to comfort a person during their process, I ask them whether the action is to help the other person or because they themselves find it too uncomfortable to be around someone in pain. It is my experience that the majority of those who interrupt the process of others have not dealt with their own feelings and issues and their suppressed pain is triggered by being around someone who is experiencing strong emotions. Because dealing with their own pain is too scary, their natural instinct is to stop another person from feeling intense emotions and thereby protect themselves from feeling their own stored trauma.

Of course it is wonderful to hug someone and show support. The timing of this, however, is extremely important. If you do it while a person is in process, it can have a very negative effect. When you do it after a person has made their breakthrough and finished their process, this same action can immensely strengthen the positive results achieved in the healing. (See 'Anchoring')

ENDING A HEALING SESSION

The way a healing session ends is extremely important. In fact, it sometimes can be the most important part of the session. If the ending is smooth and nurturing, it will reinforce and strengthen the level of healing achieved in the session and assist ongoing healing for hours or days after the session. An abrupt or sharp ending, however, can destroy all the good achieved. In extreme cases, the person may react by shutting down even more. If so, they might become afraid to face their issues or to risk another healing session.

If a healing session ends abruptly and the issue being worked with is not resolved, the person may feel violated, shamed, abandoned, betrayed, embarrassed or humiliated. This trauma could cause a person to have even more difficulty facing and accepting themself. This is especially true if you are going beyond the pure energy work and into a discussion of the underlying issues causing the energy blocks. Finishing a healing session before reaching a natural stopping point and failing to create closure with the person is much like ending a surgical operation without stitching up the person who just had the surgery.

Trust, the key to rapport, is essential in doing healing work. This is especially true where high levels of abuse or violation have occurred. Many times, especially if counselling is combined with the energy work, the person being helped may experience a great degree of vulnerability which, if the energy is shifted too quickly, can stimulate the old feelings of violation and abandonment. A healing session usually creates a bond, a closeness, a high trust level, which must be honoured and respected.

HEALING SESSION SEQUENCE

1. Discuss the reason for the session, identify the physical/emotional area to be worked upon.

2. Say opening prayer.

3. Centre and ground yourself; activate your hands.

4. Sense the energy field/check heat behind the neck.

5. Mutually agree on areas to be worked on/involve the person.

6. Draw out negative energy.
   In severe cases:
   A. Quick aura cleansing.
   B. Power-push energy out.
   C. Clap hands.
   D. Use balloon.

7. Put in positive energy.

8. Balance the body's energy as needed.

9. Run energy up the spine.

10. Do aura cleansing; when needed, seal auric field.

11. End session with discussion and a glass of water.

12. Wash hands and cleanse healing area.

GENERAL ENERGY BALANCING
NO SPECIFIC AREA TO BE WORKED ON

1. Say opening prayer.
2. Centre and ground yourself; activate your hands.
3. Sense energy field/check heat behind the neck.
4. Do rough aura cleansing.
5. Clear crown chakra.
6. Balance right/left brain.
7. Balance brow chakra.
8. Balance throat chakra.
9. Balance heart chakra.
10. Balance solar plexus chakra.
11. Balance spleen/navel chakra.
12. Balance root chakra.
13. Run energy up the spine.
14. Finish with aura cleansing; when needed, seal auric field.
15. End session with discussion and a glass of water.
16. Wash hands and cleanse healing area.

At the end of a healing session, before discussing what has taken place, hand the person a large glass of water (room temperature) and encourage them to drink it all before leaving. This will help them become more physically present and will start the release of toxins from their body.

I have found it best to allow at least 15 minutes at the end of a healing session to ask a person how they are feeling, what changes they felt and what images or realisations came up for them. I also ask if there is anything else that they wish to talk about. This process of asking questions and actively listening helps the person to get more fully in touch with their own awareness of the experience. In identifying and expressing their feelings, they bring their experience more clearly to the conscious level. Often, simply by verbalising their experience — putting it into words — the person gains greater insight. Be aware that they may not wish, or be able, to talk at that moment. Use your own intuition to check out if the person is in confusion or just calm and integrating their experience on a deep level. Let it be okay for them not to share their feelings, especially if they are not ready or are uncomfortable with it.

After a person has shared what they are feeling, give them as much positive reinforcement and feedback as possible. Pay attention to how they respond to the encouragement. If they are uncomfortable with it, back off and quietly support them by listening and by asking leading questions. Be as honest and as specific as you can with the person. Statements such as: "You did really well," "It takes a lot of courage to do what you just did," "It takes a lot of courage to face that issue," "I really want to acknowledge your willingness to feel your pain," can give a person the confidence and the courage to go further and can literally change people's lives. Statements like these are very powerful because they validate a person's healing experience and encourage them to move further into their healing process. Remember, most people have seldom had someone supporting them. This is especially true when confronting the negative energy of their abusers. Please be aware that the relationship with the healer is therapeutic in itself. The trust and support you establish may open a new doorway for further healing.

Inform the person that they may feel disoriented or different for a few hours or days as they integrate the healing energy and the changes that occur in their interaction patterns with others. I always tell the people I work with to please call me if they need to talk or if anything comes up that disturbs them. I tell them that if it is an emergency it is okay to call me any time, even in the middle of the night. In all my years of doing healing work, no one has ever called me in the middle of the night. Most of the time, just knowing that "Yes! Someone cares and is really there for me" allows a person to complete the healing process on their own.

CARE AFTER A HEALING SESSION

What a person does during the first one to three hours after a healing session can greatly support and strengthen the work done in the actual session itself. It is usually best if this period is set aside for relaxing, resting and being quiet, as well as for reflecting on the insights received in the healing session. This allows time for the healing energy to penetrate undisturbed into the body and become more fully integrated within it. Silence, soft music, journal-writing, a walk in nature or taking a nap or a hot bath can greatly enhance the healing. Loud music, crowds, meetings, intense or strenuous activity and unsupportive people are best avoided after a healing session, when a person may feel open and vulnerable.

It is also very important to drink as much water as possible during the 24 to 48 hours after a healing. This extra intake of fluids assists in removing the toxins released into the body during the healing process. If these toxins are not flushed out of the body's system, they are reabsorbed and will repollute the body. Taking a hot bath with either one cup of apple cider vinegar or one cup of epsom salts added to the water will also help the body to release toxins through the skin pores. An added benefit of the bath is that it also cleanses the aura. Apple cider vinegar and epsom salt baths may be used at any time to help cleanse the body and the body's energy field. I highly recommend taking these hot baths frequently, especially when feeling stressed, frustrated or negative.

NOTE: There are times when a person might get sick or come down with a cold after a healing session. On rare occasions this release might be quite severe and is known as a healing crisis. This reaction is caused by the shift in the person's perception, their body, their energy field and the rapid release of toxins from their body. You might wish to ask the person if they are afraid of changing or if they are grieving the loss of the old ways. Ask if they are committed to their own healing and if so encourage them to relax and surrender into releasing the old patterns. The best remedy for this is to have them rest and drink lots of water. Within a few days the person feels much better.

CLEANSING YOURSELF AND YOUR WORKPLACE

There are a number of effective techniques that can be used to cleanse yourself and your workplace on a regular basis. One technique is to visualise or sense an energy ring of golden light around the area where the healing is done so that the negative energy released is contained within a small area and does not spread out. Imagine a giant vacuum cleaner coming down from God, constantly cleansing you and your work area. See and feel the vacuum removing all of the negative energy, so that you are not bringing new people into an area that is laden with negativity and illness.

A widely accepted way to release negative energy is to wash your hands with soap and water after each and every healing session. As you do this, pray and ask that you release any and all of the negative energy and emotions that you may have picked up. Experience this negative energy flowing out of your body and into the water. Ask that all foreign energies be released from you and that you be purified before working on the next person. (See 'Releasing Excess and Negative Energy', p 158.)

Please remember to wash any towels used in a session. Be aware that the towels and tissues used have negative energy on them. Flush all tissues or deposit them directly into a waste container without touching them.

SUPPORT SYSTEMS

Support systems are the key to long-term sustained personal growth. Ongoing support can take many forms, including individual activities, group involvement and personal health care.

Personal work, such as reading books, listening to motivational tapes, eating healthy foods, exercising, praying, meditating, journal-keeping and using affirmations and visualisation can have a major impact on personal growth. If desired, much of this work can be done alone and/or in private.

Group involvement can include healthy friends, support groups, workshops and seminars. Such interaction will greatly assist in keeping your healing process and spiritual growth advancing. One of the benefits of being in a group is that you will learn from others by listening to and observing how they interact and handle situations, as well as by getting feedback about yourself.

Personal health care — including healthy eating, exercising, massage, acupuncture, chiropractic care, homoeopathic remedies, naturopathic care, colonics, herbs and the use of flower remedies — is a way of bringing the body into balance. The use of such practices will assist and support you in your healing process.

FOLLOW YOUR HEART

In this book I have described the healing techniques that have worked best for me. With each passing day, as I learn more about healing energy and understand people better, I readily modify and change the healing methods I use.

The techniques I am sharing with you in this book are not meant as absolute laws or rules, but are merely offered as a starting place for each of you on your own individual path. If what I have shared works for you, then please accept it as a gift and use it. If just the opposite works for you, then that is okay also.

In all cases when your intuition or inner knowing is guiding you to do, say or try something different, gently follow this guidance. Explore one step at a time, observing how the person you are working with responds. All learning is a process, not an end result. Please write to me c/o Findhorn Press and let me know how you are doing and what you have experienced while using these and your own techniques.

Thank you.

Appendix

READING THE BODY

HOW THE BODY COMMUNICATES

There are three main models which I rely on to gain insight into what issues a person is dealing with. In every healing I first observe the location of the negative energy and then compare it to the reference points indicated in these models. Remember that these three models are only indicators which help give insight and are never to be used as an absolute. In each case I always ask questions to check out with the person if the information provided by these reference points is accurate and applies to them. *NOTE:* There are many cases where people may be in denial or not be aware of the true cause of their pain. In such cases keep the reference points as a guide for yourself and do not try to push these people into agreeing with you if they cannot see the connection for themselves.

The first model is an observation of the upper and lower chakras; the second is an observation of the right and left sides of the body; the third is observing what specific area of the body is being affected. These models work equally well with all genders, ages, races and religions. Whenever discussing masculine or feminine energies, please remember that each person — whether male or female — embodies both types of consciousness. When these are in balance and working in harmony with each other, the person will be able to use both their right and left brain more effectively, to give and receive equally well, and will be more balanced and happy.

The first model gives insight as to whether the issue is related to the lower or higher nature of the person. When observing the upper and lower chakras, view the heart chakra as the centre separating the upper three chakras from the lower three chakras. The lower chakras represent the lower human nature. They relate to survival and power issues, emotions, sexual desires and the need for food and shelter. The upper chakras deal more with the higher nature, including love, communication, the ability to see clearly and the connection to the higher self. The balance point is the heart chakra. When the lower and upper chakras are in balance, the heart is open and fully expressing unconditional love.

Some people view the upper chakras as embodying feminine qualities and the lower chakras masculine ones. Here the heart centre perfectly balances the masculine and feminine.

The second model is to divide a person vertically and observe the right and left sides of the body. In this scenario the left side indicates the feminine, receptive qualities and the right side represents the masculine, manifestation qualities. When there are energy blocks on the left side, try to discover if they are connected to feminine energy issues such as sensitivity, spirituality, emotion, intuitiveness, receiving, nurturing, support, creativity, expressions of love or other right brain qualities.

When there are energy blocks on the right side of the body, explore whether they are connected to masculine energy issues such as protection, survival, assertiveness, manifestation, giving, logic, intellect, power and other left brain qualities.

The third model is to observe what part of the body is being affected and to see how it might relate to the issues in question.

Please review the section on 'Chakras' (pp 46-49) in addition to using the insights listed in the following section.

The way to use the following section is as a guide, so you can ask:

1. Gentle probing questions as you work with the energy.
   Example: the eyes. "Is there anything going on in your life that you would rather not look at or see?'
2. Direct questions.
   Example: the eyes. "What in your life are you unwilling to look at or afraid to see?"
   Example: the liver. "Who or what are you angry with?"
3. Open-ended questions which give the body part a voice.
   Example: "If my (*body part*) could talk, it would tell you . . . ."
   Have the person repeat the open-ended question and then allow them to answer it. Remain silent as they search for the answer. If they cannot complete the sentence immediately, have them take a deep breath and relax before asking them to repeat the question again.
   Example: "If my (heart) could speak, it would tell you (that I cannot stand the pain any longer).
4. Open-ended questions about what benefit the person is receiving from their illness.
   Example: "The benefit I get from having (*name of illness or issue*) is . . . ."

These questions can help people to get in touch with the root cause of their pain. In many cases they will break into tears as they answer.

LIST OF POSSIBLE DEEPER ISSUES

The purpose of the following section is to gain insight into the possible deeper issues behind the cause of particular illnesses. Please note that these are not to be used for diagnosis or to replace medical attention. None of the following descriptions are absolutes and sensitivity must be used when exploring possible connections. All descriptions are general in nature and must be checked out with the person you are assisting.

Accidents —
Problems with accidents are caused by anger at others or the self, feelings of helplessness and hopelessness and desire for attention. Accidents which cause pain to others stem from the need for power and control over others, anger at others or needing to punish someone. Accidents hurting only the individual are caused by anger at the self and a desire to punish and destroy the self.

Addictions —
Problems with addictions are caused by poor self-image and self-esteem, feelings of lack, insecurity, self-abuse and absence of love in our life. Addictions involve seeking something outside ourself to fulfil inner 'cravings' or to heal inner insecurities. They can be passed down from parents to children or even be a carryover from previous lifetimes.

AIDS —
Problems with AIDS are caused by anger at the self, sexual guilt, shame, poor self-image and self-esteem, feeling isolated and alone and feelings of futility. (See also Male/Female Sexual Problems.)

Allergies —
Allergies are caused by irritations with the self, with other people or with life. Most allergies stem from an earlier trauma which lowered our resistance or tolerance to the 'irritant'. When this trauma is healed, the allergic reaction will lessen or disappear.

Amnesia
Problems [illegible] ...nesia are caused by not wanting to know or

remember things from the past and not wanting to have to deal with the responsibility for living. Here it is easier to block memories out rather than risk confronting them.

Anxiety —
Problems with anxiety are caused by fear of being present or being visible and not feeling safe. "Who/what are you afraid of?" Success or failure, as well as being out of control, can trigger anxiety.

Apathy —
Problems with apathy are caused by being afraid or unwilling to be fully alive and committed to life. Apathy can stem from childhood trauma or loss. A person suffering from apathy has little or no drive or direction in life, has few strong feelings or convictions, seldom feels anger or rage and lives life from a place of futility.
(*NOTE:* For me this is the hardest type of person to assist because they are not fully committed to life or living and their emotions/ feelings are deeply suppressed.)

Arthritis —
Problems with arthritis are caused by rigid thinking and beliefs, and being afraid or unwilling to be flexible. The location of the arthritis will give clues to the areas of inflexibility in the person's thinking.

Back —
The back represents our support system. Problems with the back are caused by fears or feelings of not being supported by others. Not supporting ourselves or being afraid to support ourselves can also trigger back problems. Back pain behind the heart area is an indication of lack of love and emotional support, while pain in the lower back has to do with the lower chakra issues of survival and possible lack of financial support.

Bladder —
Problems with the bladder are caused by being 'pissed off' about something or at someone. Here anger and resentment are affecting the body's ability to eliminate toxins.

Blood Pressure –

Blood pressure represents the willingness to be in the flow of life. High blood pressure is caused by rigidity, trying to control life and unresolved/suppressed emotional pain. Low blood pressure is caused by apathy, giving up and being unwilling to participate fully in life.

Breast Problems —

Problems with the breasts are caused by becoming exhausted from nurturing and taking care of others and having little or nothing left for the self. Breast problems are a cry from the body to nurture and take care of the self.

Cancer —

Problems with cancer are caused by suppressed anger at the self or others, helplessness, irritation at something, giving up on life, feelings of futility and wanting to die. Usually the person sees no way of dealing with the situation other than by dying. In our society suicide is frowned upon, whereas dying of cancer is acceptable.

Cataracts —

Problems with cataracts are caused by being afraid or unwilling to see what is going on. As with amnesia, the person is trying to hide from the situation rather than see it clearly and deal with it.

Chronic Fatigue (ME in the UK) —

Problems with fatigue are caused by energy leakages from the auric field, feelings of hopelessness and helplessness, and the strong belief of having no control or power over one's life. Many times people with chronic fatigue have had setbacks or losses which traumatised them for a short while. Unfortunately these people have not been able fully to recover their previous strength and power after the initial setback. (*NOTE:* When working with someone with chronic fatigue make sure you surround yourself with intense white light and protect yourself first. Start the energy balancing with a rough aura cleansing, then a general energy balancing. Finish with a thorough aura cleansing and sealing of the aura).

Colds —

Problems with colds are caused by not giving the body the nutrition and rest it desires, falsely believing that everyone gets colds, and wanting love and attention. Some people will only allow themselves permission to slow down and take a rest when they are sick. Colds are also a way of releasing and healing.

Depression –

Problems with depression are caused by being afraid or unwilling to live life fully, feelings of helplessness and the faulty belief that we don't have the power to change our life. Depression is also caused by anger turned inward at the self which is trapped in the body. (See also Chronic Fatigue)

Diabetes —

Problems with diabetes are caused by a lack of sweetness in one's life. The pancreas, which controls diabetes, is also the organ associated with psychic energy. Check for attitudes and beliefs about love, joy, happiness and psychic energy.

Ears —

Ears represent the willingness to hear. Problems with the ears are caused by being afraid to hear or to listen — or by struggling to hear.

Eyes —

Eyes represent the willingness to see clearly. Problems with the eyes are caused by being afraid or unwilling to look at or see what is really going on. A near-sighted person is more willing to see what is directly in front of them and less willing to see things further away (such as the future). This type of person might also be self-focused. A far-sighted person is more willing to see things further out and less willing to see things right in front of them. This type of person might be more future-oriented and less willing to look at themself.

Fatigue —

See Chronic Fatigue

Feet —
Feet represent the willingness to be self-reliant, to stand firm and to be grounded. Problems with the feet are caused by being afraid or unwilling to be supported or to support oneself. They may also stem from fear of standing one's ground or of stepping out. The feet are also symbolic of 'under-standing'. Flat feet represent not feeling supported by the universe.

Female Sexual Problems —
Female problems can be caused by being afraid or unwilling lovingly to embrace being a female. This can stem from anger and resentment against the female body, about being a woman, against other women or against living in a male-dominated society. Feelings of inadequacy, shame, sexual guilt or rejection can affect female sexuality. Problems can also be caused by the feminine energy being out of balance, denying or fearing one's power or — at the other extreme — fearing and denying one's gentleness and ability to love. Problems also arise from the belief that women are controlled by men and therefore have no real power in life. Female problems are sometimes an act of rebellion against the self, a parent or one's sexual partner.

Frigidity —
Problems with frigidity are caused by imbalances in the hormones oestrogen and progesterone, or anger at the self or the sexual partner. Many times this can also stem from anger at the parent of the opposite sex. (See also Female and Male Sexual Problems).

Hands —
Hands represent the willingness to reach out, touch and grasp life. Problems with the hands are caused by being afraid or unwilling to receive (left hand) or to give to life (right hand).

Headaches —
Problems with headaches are caused by being afraid or unwilling to trust the process of life and by over-thinking, over-analysing and attempting to control life by figuring it out. Trying to understand what is happening and why it is happening is less important than how we react to life.

Heart –
The heart represents the willingness to love. Problems with the heart are caused by being afraid or unwilling to trust love openly. This could stem from childhood pain, abuse or fear of being hurt.

Hips —
Hips represent a willingness to move forward. Problems with the hips are caused by being afraid or unwilling to move forward in life.

Insomnia —
Problems with insomnia are caused by being afraid or unwilling to let go and trust the process of life. Insomnia arises from attempting to hold on to and control life, and by feelings of not being supported. Insomnia can also be caused by recurring nightmares or memories of childhood abuse, usually sexual, starting to surface. (*NOTE:* The person might not even be conscious of this until you ask probing questions. Carefully review the section on 'The Hierarchy of Pain and Protection' and 'Shutdown' before working with insomnia.)

Jaws —
Problems with the jaw are caused by suppressed, unverbalised anger and resentment. The expressions 'gritting one's teeth' or 'clenching one's jaw' clearly demonstrate the actions associated with this.

Kidneys —
Problems with the kidneys are caused by fear. When the fear level in the body rises the kidneys are affected. The kidneys can also hold on to and store fear — such as fear of self-expression, fear of others or fear of life.

Knees —
Knees represent the willingness to surrender to a higher purpose. Problems with the knees are caused by being afraid or unwilling to surrender the ego and personality.

Legs —
Legs represent a willingness to step out and move forward. Problems with the legs are caused by being afraid or unwilling to do

this. They can also arise from feelings of not being supported on one's path either by others or by the self. (See also Feet)

Liver —
Problems with the liver are caused by anger. When the anger level in the body rises, the liver is affected. The liver can also hold on to and store anger. This could be caused by anger at the self, at others or at life.

Lungs —
Lungs represent the willingness to take in the breath of life. Problems with the lungs or breathing are caused by being afraid or unwilling to experience life fully or to take in all that life offers.

Male Sexual Problems —
Male problems are caused by being afraid or unwilling lovingly to embrace being a male. This can stem from anger and resentment toward the male body, toward being a male, toward other men or toward living in a male-dominated society. Feelings of inadequacy, shame, sexual guilt and rejection can affect male sexuality. Problems can also be caused by the masculine energy being out of balance or denying or fearing one's power or — at the other extreme — fearing or denying one's gentleness and ability to love. Male problems can also be an act of rebellion against the self, a parent or one's sexual partner.

Mouth —
The mouth represents the willingness to take in nourishment and to speak our truth. Problems with the mouth are caused by being afraid or unwilling to take in nourishment or to communicate our needs, feelings and desires. (See also Throat)

Neck —
Problems with the neck are caused by being afraid or unwilling to be flexible. The term 'stiff-necked' aptly describes this rigidity and holding on to our ideas and thoughts. Holding on to our head causes stiffness and inflexibility.

Nose —
The nose represents the willingness to take in the fragrance of life. Problems with the nose are caused by being afraid or

unwilling to smell certain odours. This could stem from unresolved traumas involving odours or irritation with the smell of life or with our environment. Problems can be caused by odours which were present when early childhood or birth trauma was experienced.

Sexual Disease —
Problems with sexual disease are caused by sexual guilt, shame, self-punishment and anger towards others, especially the parent of the opposite sex or one's partner.

Shoulders —
Problems with the shoulders are caused by an unwillingness to trust the process of life. The shoulders carry life burdens. When the burdens get too heavy or cannot be released, we can feel angry, trapped, frustrated and resentful. Feelings of futility, hopelessness and helplessness can also result from prolonged frustration.

Stomach —
The stomach represents the willingness to digest food and new ideas. Problems with the stomach are caused by being afraid or unwilling to receive nutrition or to digest new ideas.

Teeth —
Problems with the teeth are caused by being afraid or unwilling to sink our teeth into life or from gritting our teeth and not speaking out. Fear of living life fully and biting off a chunk of life (or a project) can keep us on the outside of living. Fear of expressing our anger, resentment, desires or needs also keeps us isolated.

Throat —
The throat represents the willingness to communicate. Problems with the throat are caused by being afraid or unwilling to communicate or verbalise our needs, desires and fears. Problems with the throat are caused by swallowing our words and choking on them. (See also Mouth)

Tongue —
Problems with the tongue are caused by being afraid or unwilling to taste life fully and to speak our truth. The tongue is designed to taste the flavours of life and to communicate feelings, needs and desires.

Weight Problems —
Weight represents the willingness to be present in life and to stay in balance. Problems with weight are caused by unresolved emotional trauma, sexual abuse, being out of control and poor self-image and self-esteem. Excess weight can result from fear of starvation or not having enough food, protection against sexual advances by making the body less attractive or by insulating it against emotional pain. Abnormally low weight can result from fear of being fully alive, fear of criticism for being overweight, fear of nurturing and nourishing the self and the need to have power and be in control over something.

INDEX